Prayer

and

Peanut Butter

by

Shirley Lueth

Copyright© 1978 by Shirley Lueth

Aurora News-Register
Publishing Co.
Aurora, Nebr. 68818

ISBN 0-8300-2129-9

i

TABLE OF CONTENTS

FOREWORD

Somewhere, sometime, someone said . . . "If you must write
. . . write about something you know best . . ."

I'd dearly love to write a 765 page novel on a torrid affair in
the swamps of Louisiana with vivid descriptive words
complete with a clandestine meeting between two champion
lovers . . . but I'm afraid a picnic in Streeter Park wouldn't
stir the juices of anyone.

We are not members of the Jet Set. I have met no Queens nor
dined with Kings. My "roots" include fruit farmers and funeral
directors. I don't drink enough to write about alcoholism
and I am certainly not going to write about sex!

Oh, I know about sex . . . yes, I do! But I am not going to tell
what I know. I feel that's one thing everyone should find out
for themselves. I don't think you should read about it in a
book. Experience is the best teacher, I always say.

I am neither famous or infamous. In fact, if you want to know
the truth, I'm pretty all-around dull. I am not much of an expert
on anything. I definitely cannot write a "how-to" book. I really
do not know "how-to" do anything much . . .

Except to be a mother!

Now, it is obvious that in this day and age no one sits down
and plans on having seven children. It just happens.

I tell the children when they ask . . . and they do . . . that God
looked down and chose us to be their parents. Sometimes they
are not pleased with His choice. Sometimes their Dad and I are
not too thrilled either.

But we wouldn't change a birth certificate. Not one! And
they can't! So we are stuck together . . . with prayer and peanut
butter . . . forever and ever and ever.

Prayer and Peanut Butter was born at the Aurora News-
Register and adopted by the Grand Island Daily Independent.
It is a semi-truthful history of our family.

MOTHERS ARE NOT HARD TO SPOT!

I can pinpoint a mother right away. Not only can I tell that she is a mother but usually, 99 times out of 100, I can give you the ages of her children. This is a skill I have acquired in the past 20-odd years . . . it is not something I went to school for, took a correspondence course for or studied from an expert. It is called raw experience.

For instance — the mother of a six week old baby is interchangeably starry-eyed and sleepy-eyed. She is very seldom seen fashionably without a diaper bag or socially outside of the doctor's office.

The two-to-five-year old group mother has a perpetual outstretched right arm . . . stiffened at the joint. She has used this arm to guide hundreds of little feet across miles of streets and sidewalks and to brace small bodies in the car when it brakes to a stop at intersections. Ordinarily she has at least one tendril of hair escaping down the back of her neck.

Mothers of five to ten year olds have a fixation about scotch tape. She can be found in any variety store lingering wistfully over the school supply counter looking at all of that scotch tape right out there in the open that no one can misplace, unwind or use to tape the cat's mouth shut. Conversations center around praise and condemnation of elementary school teachers and the merits of the Brady Bunch vs. the Partridge Family.

There is a slight pause now . . . a cooling off period . . . during the 10-to-12 year old age where the mother is slightly hard to spot. The child has become fairly independent but comes home for dinner on time and goes to bed before 10 p.m. It has almost reached an ideal stage. The mother looks fairly normal and the child usually leaves her pretty much alone unless he needs money.

This is the age that finds a mother sometimes deciding it is time she should have a hobby like golf, bridge or needlepoint. She can use a hobby. She is approaching the teen years. She needs all the help she can get.

Mothers of teen-agers are by far the easiest to spot. They look sort of numb. All over. They've gone from the six-week old starry-eyed to the sixteen-year old glassy-eyed category. They have turned into professional debators over-night. Skirt hems, hair lengths and curfew take up so much of their time they no longer have time for the hobbies they pursued for that

1

fleeting two years.

There are four teen-agers in our house. I'm not only glassy-eyed, numb and a professional debator but a few other categories I'd rather not mention in a family book.

I could have never survived all those years and all those stages without Prayer and Peanut Butter. I have discovered you can not raise kids without them.

VERY WICKED PLANS FOR RETIREMENT

Some people have marvelous plans for their retirement. Some want to travel, some to fish, some to garden or collect things, read historical novels or just sit around a lot and eat. My husband has picked five out of these six things. I plan to live with our children.

One at a time . . . three months here, three months there . . . I plan to spend time with each one. I can hardly wait. I have a fabulous list of things that I will pack in my big suitcase and take with me. Each day I add something new. The list is growing and growing.

So far I plan to take old sweaty tennis shoes (to wear in public with my good dresses); 20 pair of torn and raveled blue jeans (to wear INSTEAD of my good dresses most of the time); 86 pair of socks (one each); 14 bottles of shampoo (all expensive and without lids); 1000 empty pop bottles (to roll under my bed); 1,800 gum wrappers (woven in a chain to drape over the living room chair with a sign that says "Hands Off - This Means YOU!")

I'm also going to take 19 purses (eventually to be left somewhere — preferably no closer to home than 70 miles); 12 sets of jacks (to scatter indiscriminately around carpeted floors to surprise all those who walk in the dark — at night — barefoot!); down slips from the Senior Citizen Center; three guitars; one stereo (LOUD); one million Lawrence Welk records (LOUD — Well, as LOUD as Lawrence Welk can get); 17 leaf collections (crumbly); 14 stamp collections (expensive); a gigantic beer can collection (unwashed and still smelling); one bug collection (that's all I could stand — enough is enough); 23 stray puppies and kitties (all female with fleas and needing shots) and the normal amount of wadded paper, fingerprints, wet glass rings, overdue library books, pretzels and popcorn to scatter about here and there to make their homes "comfortable and lived in."

I have many things in mind that will make the time pass

quickly while spending my alloted time at each home — little things that I have stored up over the years. I do not think time will hang heavy on my hands.

Naturally, I will get up very early. I must make every minute count. I have many things to do. And I will have a bicycle — a 10-speed bicycle with a perpetual flat tire. When the tire is conveniently not flat I will ride it everywhere — very fast and over and through flower beds and newly-seeded lawns . . . except I will not ride it on my paper route. Oh yes, I plan to have a paper route, a route that is located many, many blocks away from my current home — a paper route that involves days and days of snow, rain and gales of wind. I think I will probably have a morning route so that everyone can get up bright and early every morning (especially on Sunday) and join in all the fun. We will make it a family project and I will get all of the money.

I can't wait to sell Girl Scout cookies. Hundreds and hundreds of boxes of them. I will eat one cookie out of each box that has to be delivered to friends, relatives or neighbors. I will not touch or mutilate the boxes that must be taken to people that are never home.

I will keep my diary, notes from my friends, old flowers, bubble gum cards, comic books, rubber bands, rusty nails, photographs, empty boxes, frayed shoe strings, barrettes, tennis balls, golf balls and dice in my dresser drawers. My underwear, I will lay on a chair — or on the floor — or under the bed.

Most of my waking hours will be spent in the bathroom or pounding on the bathroom door yelling "Get Out — Get Out!" and drawing pictures in the dust on top of the refrigerator and dialing numbers at random on the telephone.

I'll order every free thing offered in the magazine and stuff "win a prize" boxes at the county fair with my host's name and hide ballpoint pens and beg for nickels.

I'll outgrow my swimsuit (well, that's really nothing new . . . I do that every year anyway . . . I sure don't have to go live with anyone to do that!) and will decorate my bedroom with pizza crust. I might even streak. And then again I might not!

I've been so excited about my plans to live with our children after retirement that I can hardly sleep nights. But it hasn't been all roses. There's some work involved too. After all, I've been a m-o-t-h-e-r too long. It's hard for me to throw habits away. I have to practice.

I have to practice how to go limp in multiple ways when it is time to do dishes and to roll my eyes and stick my finger in my nose when introduced to strangers and wear my socks until the pores stop up and to kick people under the table without being detected.

3

Just the other night I tried that one and caught my husband's shins by mistake. I thought there for a minute that I might have to find a new home before my retirement. But he soon settled down. He usually does. Well, sometimes he does. He only mentioned it 14 times throughout the evening. That's not so bad.

Anyway, there's one of our children in particular that I can't wait to live with. I think perhaps he will be first. You see, to him, a soggy potato chip dropped on the living room floor equates our home environment as ghetto status. The fact that HE dropped it has nothing to do with it. The fact that I did not immediately pick it up does. He gave me a broom for Mother's Day. Get the image? And he's the one that spends three-fourths of the year among dormitory debris.

Well, there had better not be a molecule of dust in HIS house when I live there or I will nag and turn up my nose at the furniture and call people long distance on the telephone. If I could I'd grow a beard . . . wouldn't that surprise him?

When I live with one of them I will cry all of the time — that's it — just cry. When they say "good morning, dear mother, how are you?" I will burst into tears and run to my room and only come out at meal time. Days will go by before they will see me without tears streaming down my face.

One or two will find me, during my waking hours, on the floor, wrapped in a blanket, in front of the television. We will not communicate except during commercials, when my main topic of conversation will be "Huh?" . . . "It's not my turn" . . . "Let HER do it for a change," and "Why do you always pick on me?"

One of them will never, never know where I am. I will only show up to fill the clothes hamper and eat.

Shopping could be the biggest adventure of all — for all of us. I plan to dash up and down the supermarket aisles yelling "Buy me . . . buy me" . . . and "Can I have a penny for the gumball machine!" I will yell very loud — so that every head will turn and everyone will look and everyone will think "Well, if I was that child . . . I'd certainly spank that mother!" I will do this every day. It will be fun.

I also plan to peek under dressing room doors while in large department stores. I haven't practiced this one yet. I'm afraid to. I figure this one will have to be spontaneous.

In nearly every house I live in I will scatter baby powder in the bathroom. I will put it behind the door, on the curtains, in the sink and all over the walls. It will be very thick and very hard to wash off and then I will say I didn't do it . . . even though the baby powder has my name on it and it is laying on the floor beside my bed.

I will learn to stand patiently at the elbow of my current host

4

or hostess when he or she has company and wants to converse in private. I will never leave the room or that person's side even if a hurricane is occurring outside or someone rushes in with a million dollars or Santa Claus is coming down the chimney. Nothing could be as exciting as the conversation that is going on . . . especially when I know that I'm not wanted anywhere near. I will do this a lot and watch my host turn red in the face and try to bribe me to leave. I will sometimes accept the bribe — if it is over a dollar.

Oh yes, I am full of plans. My husband laughs and says . . . "You'll never do it?" I laugh back and say "Oh, I might." The children just tremble.

But there is just one thing. I haven't had one good concrete invitation to live with anyone. I can't imagine why. Can you?

A FEAR OF MECHANICAL THINGS

I'll tell you . . . it's really something to get up, face a new day and know your coffee pot is smarter than you are. It gives you the self-confidence needed to make the whole day a success.

We used to have the old-fashioned kind of coffee pot that human error didn't affect. Make a mistake and you just had a pot of lousy coffee. Now we have the new kind that filters, keeps the water in its top, has little red buttons that flash and a container that takes up three-fourths of the counter space in the kitchen.

Just the other morning I made a mistake. My mind is not at calculator sharpness at 6 a.m. I put the water in the wrong place. The little red buttons flashed, the tank gurgled and the bottom of the container began to crackle. I thought it was going to blow up. I ran to wake my husband.

"Help me! help me!" I shouted in his ear. "The coffee pot is going crazy!"

"Oh, Lord," he said. "You can't be afraid of a coffee pot. A mouse, I can understand. But a coffee pot?"

He did get up to help me, however, no matter how silly he thought it was. He knew I had thrown the old coffee pot away; the old coffee pot that I never washed, that never failed and never spit and groaned when I plugged it in. He knew he would get hot water for breakfast if he didn't get up.

He immediately saw the problem, reversed the water, plugged it in, turned it on and the little red buttons smiled. The coffee dripped away. Everything was fine.

Appliances always work funny for me. For one thing, I'm scared to death of them. I think they know it, too. I have a pressure cooker that I operate from behind the kitchen door. Did you ever try cooking dinner while standing six feet away from the stove? It isn't easy.

But, my goodness, that pressure cooker is lethal. It sputters and that tiny pointed thing hops up and down and it splatters and sprews water and right before it quits cooking, the pot sort of shudders and the whole thing quivers.

I have quiet spiritual communication with my Maker every time I cook stew. When I go . . . I certainly don't care to go with mashed carrots all over my face.

Recently a whole new appliance entered my life in the form of a curling iron. When one is expecting a new mink, a jeweled necklace or, at least, a gold watch, a curling iron can be a letdown.

I named it "Curly." What else?

Well, the first thing old "Curly" and I had to do was have an understanding. I had to understand how to operate her and she had to understand she was not to burn my neck.

The directions said "CAUTION: Use only 120 volts, 60 cycle, AC current." I didn't know what that meant. Suppose I plugged it in the wrong socket and it melted in my head? My husband said it was OK, that I could use the bathroom plug. He was the one who gave me the curling iron (and the coffee pot) and although I never quite know what he has in mind . . . I have to trust someone.

I practiced with old "Curly" while she was cold . . . just like the directions said. I learned to isolate the strand of hair, hold the section by the ends, clamp old "Curly" around the roots and slide the rod perfectly.

Next I had to pick a style. Did I want waves, page-boy, tendrils or marcel. These were my choices. I did not want to end up looking like a wavy lady-of-the-night. I wanted something soft, suave and sweet. I thought sure I could accomplish this. Old "Curly" and I understood each other.

I plugged her in, murmuring encouraging noises when she balked at split-ends. My hand grew numb from clamping the end of the iron. In fact, my palm was sweating and the rod was slipping dangerously. My palm always sweats when I'm nervous. And I was nervous.

Things weren't going right at all. Quite often I was getting the whole thing tied in a knot and I was beginning to smoke. I hadn't read anything in the directions about smoking . . . or smelling.

When I unplugged old "Curly," I had two slashes across my cheek, one finger that was charred and my hair looked like a sheep's.

6

But I will try her again tomorrow . . . just as soon as I figure out how I can stand behind the bathroom door and use a curling iron.

GYM BAGS RAISE AN AWFUL STINK!

With my past experience, there is little doubt in my mind that the first assignment I will get the day I step into heaven will be the laundry room. I can only hope that angels don't carry their dirty wings around in gym bags.

Mothers who have raised nothing but girl children don't know what they have missed. They haven't really pushed life's little experiences over the edge until they have opened up a five-day-old gym bag in an air-tight utility room.

The first time I did this our cat inhaled once, threw up and disappeared for three days.

I'm not going into detail about the contents of a gym bag. You that have faced them on Saturday morning are well aware of what they contain. The rest of you can remain in blessed innocence.

School and gym bags are synonymous. The minute physical education appears on the school curriculum the mother-of-a-son has a life that contains three positive things she can look forward to . . . death, taxes and smelly gym socks.

Instinctively, for survival, I worked out a system:

I intercept the gym bag on the afternoon it arrives home from school. Outside. In the fresh air. As far from the house as possible but still not across property lines.

I leave it out under the stars all night. With the zipper open.

I don't even think about rain. For one thing a little wet rain can only help the situation and as for worrying about mildew forming . . . it can't! And there is always the outside chance that someone might steal it. They won't — but I can always hope.

Posting it outside has other advantages. A ripe gym bag is as good a deterrent for prowlers as two Doberman pinschers, a German shepherd with fangs and a five-alarm burglar system. It also keeps away unexpected drop-in-callers who feel like a snack when you have only peanut butter and jelly in the house.

I have noticed with some bitterness that the mothers-of-all-girls have time over the weekend to play bridge, shop, get their hair fixed and prepare gourmet meals for their families. I spend most of Saturday trying to deodorize and disinfect and Sundays attempting to track down the smells I missed on Saturday.

On the other hand, I can think of one thing worse. Multiply your particular, personal gym bags by the boy population at the school and think of that locker room along about Thursday at 6 p.m. There is justice in the world after all . . .

I'd rather be a mother than a P.E. teacher.

A HOLIDAY KITCHEN CATASTROPHE

Traditions are made to be broken I always tell my family. Even Thanksgiving ones. They do not argue anymore. They accept oatmeal cookies and whipped cream for Thanksgiving dessert without asking any questions. In fact, it has become a tradition.

I tried to make a holiday pie . . . I really did. I wanted to be the type of mother they would all want to travel "over the hills and through the woods" to see on Thanksgiving Day. I wanted to be the type of mother that would inspire conversations around the fireplace about the "good old days" and Mom's pumpkin pies. So far, they all come by Interstate and sit around talking about fumbles and football games. Or they talk about the first pumpkin pie I DID try to make.

I should have known better. I should have known that just because my oatmeal cookies didn't stick to the cookie tin more than 50 per cent of the time that this did not mean I could whip out a perfect pie the first time — or the second — or the third. I was defeated from the minute I opened the cookbook to Pastries-Pie Crust.

God, it looked so simple . . . and turned out to be so hard. I mean, how can you foul up shortening, flour, water and a pinch of salt? Let me tell you how!

First of all you do not take large globs of shortening and plunk it in a bowl, willy-nilly. You measure. Correctly. You do not measure as if you are determining the moisture content of corn. You do not place water in the measuring cup and throw in shortening until the water level flows over the rim of the cup. It is not a favorable way to work with pie crust. Drowned shortening loses its crumble.

Tossing soggy shortening in a bowl, I went to the "mixing in the flour" step. Another misinterpretation of the recipe. I didn't have enough flour. I couldn't get my hands out of the bowl. I had mixed up a glue that would put Elmer to shame. My hands stuck to the sides of the bowl. I was afraid it was going to dry and I would be encased in concrete mittens forever.

I screamed. I was all alone. Except for Augie Doggie. He came bounding into the kitchen.

"Don't just stand there," I yelled, "dump in more flour."

He licked my foot. I was on my own. Working one muffled hand free, I tried to flex my fingers. They were frozen in goo. Managing to free a finger, I unloaded a blast of flour that could have covered an acre — almost. It sifted down around the bowl, covering my still stuck hand, a portion of the bowl, the counter top, my bosom, the floor and Augie Doggie.

"Serves you right," I muttered. He flew out of the kitchen like a big, white, hairy ghost. The cat took one look, clung to the curtains and entered the first stages of a cat cardiac arrest.

But I had no time for cat problems. The cat was going to have to get out of this one alone. I had a pie crust to make. I faced the mountain of shortening and flour with false courage. It heaped up over the edges of the bowl. At this moment I had enough ingredients for 72 pies with strips of crust left over.

I plunged both hands in and began to knead the dough. In the back of my mind I vaguely remembered hearing some-where that you did knead bread dough but definitely avoided doing it to pie crust. But I had no time for trivia. Besides, I had no choice. I certainly couldn't delicately approach and pick at the mess facing me. It would take six months just to sort it.

9

So I jumped right in there and labored — with all my might. My fingers began to wear out. My elbows were going fast and an ache appeared around my neck and shoulders. For 15 minutes I punched and pummeled that dough. It was the consistency of dirty clay. I hated, with all my heart, every pilgrim I had ever known.

At this point I didn't think it mattered how much salt I put in — so I pinched a bunch. I felt better. The recipe called for water. I drank the first glass. I needed it far worse than the pie crust. I couldn't see how the water was going to help at this point but I poured it in. It settled in a puddle on top and stayed there. I could see my reflection. I didn't look too good.

Gathering it on top of the table, I attacked with the rolling pin. I rolled and rolled and rolled.

"Flatten out!" I shouted. The dog and cat hit the floor.

Suddenly the pie crust wrapped itself around the rolling pin. It clung with all its might. I could not pry it loose.

"That's it," I said calmly. With careful calculation and direct aim I threw the rolling pin encased in pie crust at the nearest wall. It smashed into the woodwork, jarred the light fixtures and fell with a thud to the floor. I left it there and took a nap.

My family didn't say a thing when I served oatmeal cookies piled high with whipped cream that Thanksgiving. One or two even said it was the best Thanksgiving dinner we ever had.

I thought that was nice, don't you?

DIET IS SPELLED H-U-N-G-R-Y

For the past 10 years I have dieted. Off and on I have lost about two full grown adults. And gained three.

I'm back at it again . . . and I can tell you folks, I'm hungry. Don't let these professional hard-boiled-egg-eaters tell you any different; ice cream is NOT poison, chocolate will NOT make a 46-year-old break out and dieting is NOT fun. It doesn't make me feel vibrant, vigorous and vivacious. It makes me churlish, crusty and curt. I barely get by the morning without wanting to french fry the cat.

This time, however, I'm not doing it alone. My husband, too, is trying to lose weight. But he's doing it with character. He doesn't talk about it . . . just gnaws on turnips and drinks iced tea without complaining at all. Not a word. He doesn't pass his hand across his stomach and say, "I'm cramping . . . hand me the peanut butter," nor does he sneak into the little girls' room and steal their candy corn. He can pass the refrigerator without passionately consuming the butter dish and he doesn't ask strangers on the street for food.

"How do you do it?" I asked him as I knelt on the floor looking under the couch for something to eat.

"Just don't think about it. Eating is all in your mind."

"How come mine is all in my stomach? Look, all I've eaten for days is carrots and I still appear to be a pregnant rabbit. My ears are even growing. I don't think it is supposed to work like this."

"You aren't exercising," he answered, jogging around the room and stopping before me with four push-ups.

Personally, exercises bore me stiff. I see no reason in the world for working up more appetite than I have now. After a rousing session of bends and squats I'm hungrier than before and start hanging around Augie-Doggie's dish. He used to be such a friendly dog but now that I'm dieting he's become quite cheeky. He places a protective paw over his food whenever I come near.

I glanced over the dog food bag the other day when he wasn't looking and according to my weight and the feeding instructions I would be eligible to eat about 10 to 15 cups of his food per day. I only get ¼ cup of cottage cheese, ½ cup of peas and two tablespoons of gravy on my diet. That's not very much. I think I could get used to eating Ash and Soybean Meal. And it has vitamin B12. The sack says so.

Augie likes it. And he's a smart dog. What's more, he is not very fat . . . hairy, but not fat. I need bulk to make me happy and I think dog food might do it. I could always add catsup.

What I really need is something to propel me out of the kitchen. I don't know why someone doesn't invent a big hand that would grab me by the throat every time I open a bread sack.

"Will Power, honey, that's what you need!" my husband said, nibbling on a bean sprout. "Elevate your mind to higher things."

I tried. I honestly did. I told him about the size 14 lounging pajamas I saw in the store. They cost $89.00. That wasn't what he had in mind when he talked about higher things, he said.

I do have to admit I am tired of buying my clothes in the tent and awning department. Just once I'd like to buy something without elastic — something that buttons and zips without chewing flesh — something that belts without binding. I want something that skims on without throttling and something that has darts. Why, I haven't worn darts for years. I'm not even sure I remember what they look like.

I do not expect thin people to know what I am talking about. I do not expect those people who can turn their backs on creamed corn to have the slightest idea what it is like to be the type of person whose germs weigh six ounces each. I catch cold and gain 12 pounds.

I do not expect thin people to understand how overweights form attachments to their bathroom scales. I do not expect them to understand why I talk to my scale.

"Good morning, scale ... how do you feel today? Are you tired of sitting under the sink? Would you like to move into the living room? Would you like a new chenille cover? How about a racy pink? Would that make you feel light and airy?"

I do not expect thin people to understand why I want to jump up and down on my scale and smash it into the floorboards, chenille cover and all, when it arrows up so swiftly and quickly and so high.

But I'll do it this time. I really will. In six months you won't know me.

Just in case you don't ... I'll be the one hanging around the dog food factory with a catsup bottle in my hand.

DETASSELING TIME

Who is the child on the living room floor, sacked out like a lump of dirty clay? Who is the child that is barely breathing and has a worn and wrinkled plastic bag clutched in its fist? Who is the child that Augie-Doggie sniffs and rejects? Who is the child?

The child is a detasseler, earning gobs of spending money for future county fairs.

Who is the apparition behind the wheel of the car? Who is the phantom-of-the-early morning with closed eyes, driving down the highway? Who is that, dressed in her nightgown, not nodding to acquaintances, not waving, not wanting to be recognized and definitely not wanting a flat tire?

It is the mother of the detasseler, delivering her little workman to his embarkation point.

Who is that snoring on the bed? Who is that lying there, peacefully sleeping away the dawning of the new day, oblivious to the outer world and its early morning dew and rotten sunrise? Who is it that said, "If you are going to get up that early, ride your bike or stay home!" Who is it that stifles young enterprise?

It is the father of the detasseler. I bet you guessed that. He is sleeping through his child's first broad steps into the world of business. He is lucky. And smart. And not tired.

Personally, I am grateful to the seed companies. There is nothing that takes the spark out of a 13-year-old like eight hours in the cornfield. I didn't always know this. When our oldest daughter was approaching the age of detasseling I heard . . . and believed . . . that a worker had to be 15 and stand at least 5 feet tall. She was 14 years, 11½ months and stood 4 feet 11 inches in her stocking feet. I wouldn't let her sign up. She cried and cried.

That's all changed. It changed when I learned how marvelous a summer job for children can be. I began to brainwash our eight-and nine-year-olds in the late spring.

"Look old," I said, "and stretch tall. Maybe you can earn lots of money for Barbie doll clothes or a new tricycle if we can fool the straw boss."

We couldn't and down deep I don't think I wanted to, but when they did reach the legal age and height to enlist in the corn corps I did not hesitate to encourage them.

All of our children have detasseled. Well, not the oldest . . . she never did make it. Some worked longer than others. The shortest record was reached by a son. He didn't even make it on the back of the truck. Took one look at the machete in the hands of the school bully and decided wandering through crowded cornfields in fear of his life was not the way he wanted to spend a sunny summer day, money or no money.

The best record, so far, is being held by the current detasseler. She hasn't missed at all and hasn't complained once. Of course, she's only been at it one day.

Anyone who thinks supplying a child's social security number and signing the permit slip ends the total connection with that detasseler has things worked out a lot better than I do.

Heavens, I have spent a small fortune just in providing the proper lunch box and thermos bottle. Gone are the days when the kids grab a brown paper bag and a jar of water. It has to have class . . . and be made of styrofoam.

They covet their dad's expensive cooler.

"If I had that," they say wistfully, turning so their sunburn reflects off the wall, "I could take watermelon. Johnny Jones takes watermelon. He also has fried chicken, cold tomatoes and potato salad. He says my jelly sandwich draws corn borers."

I don't believe that. They have insecticides for corn borers don't they?

"Mark my words," I warn, "Johnny Jones will end up with ptomaine. He won't last the season. There you will be . . . rich . . . and he will just be sick."

I am picky about ptomaine. I won't let them take tuna, egg

13

salad, luncheon meats or cheeses. This limits them to peanut butter and jelly and if this provides a snack for borers, I'm sorry, I'm not going to poison my child. I tell them they can put on cucumbers to spice it up and add variety. They go yuck and continue to covet the cooler.

In ideal homes, the detasseler is provided his or her own alarm. It is set for 5:30 and kids get up in ample time to arise happily, dress properly and eat a substantial breakfast.

In our house the alarm clock belongs to mother and is weak. So is mother. But I gain amazing strength as I call "get up" for the 14th time. A lot of strength. I adore starting out the day in a rage. My adrenal glands get such a workout during this period they could sleep all winter if they wanted to. They usually don't. Something always comes up to get them going.

But everything evens out . . . and problems are forgotten . . . when the first check arrives. Suddenly child is richer than parents. The check is propped on the TV for everyone to see and admire. It is not cashed for 24 hours. It is too precious. It has been an "experience." A good one.

Now their father and I know they are capable of supporting us in our old age — as long as the corn tassels.

IF YOU THINK YOU HAVE PROBLEMS NOW
WAIT UNTIL YOU HAVE CARPETING.

Why do housewives think that wall-to-wall carpeting will solve all their problems?

I'm no different than anyone else. Several years ago it came to my attention that our home needed a boost . . . a big boost. I suggested w-w carpeting. My husband suggested I scrub and wax the floors we had. He felt the results might amaze me.

But this did not end my campaign. I can be very determined . . . in many, different ways. I cried a lot, begged some, threatened, complained of headaches and swollen ankles and generally became very, very nervous to live with.

I think he got tired of my martyred and nervous attitude, so he said, "Maybe." Well, this was as good as "yes" in my book. I looked in the yellow pages and called the nearest carpet man.

He was a handsome and persuasive salesman, this carpet man. He smiled pleasantly, patted the children on the head and talked quietly and expertly about such things as weave, quality, nap, threads, fabric and the practicability of carpeting over any other kind of floor covering.

The handsome and persuasive salesman even hinted that our marriage might improve if we got rid of all those cold, bare floors. He smiled knowingly. I didn't really know what he meant. But I was willing to take his word. He was some salesman.

But he didn't tell me that his carpet layer was a snob! After we moved all of the furniture into the kitchen and waited for three days, mashed in by innersprings and clothes hampers, he finally DID show up — and acted as if he had just finished carpeting the entire first floor of the Vatican and our house sure was a come-down and "could you take the little boy outside before he swallows all the tacks" and "I do not answer questions while I work."

I tried to fade out of the background and kept busy in the kitchen straightening dresser drawers, keeping the little boy out of the tacks and restraining my mouth. I gradually grew used to keeping unbroken silence from 8 'til 5, but it was particularly hard on the children. They had to stay outside a lot. Occasionally, I let them in for food.

I jumped every time the phone rang. I tried to ignore it altogether, for in order to answer it, I had to cross the Carpet King's path. I also had to cross his path to go to the bathroom. This was probably my severest problem.

Perhaps he was skillful in his job . . . he kept telling me he was. But he sure was slow. And besides, his young, blackhaired assistant (who whispered to me one day, after obtaining permission for a drink of water, that he was married and had three children) did all the heavy work. The King just sat back on his heels and complained about having to carpet houses that were no bigger than the hen house on his farm in the hills.

He left one day . . . just as silently as he came. He just gathered up his hammer, his carpet-pusher to the waller, his hamper full of nails, tacks and lunch, his attitude that I would never be the type to appreciate nice things, his poor blackhaired assistant with the three children, and left.

And he left all the closet doors flat on the floor. Every one of them. I had w-w carpeting all right, but not one door was on its hinges. I called the store. I asked for the handsome salesman. I told him I wanted my doors back on their hinges. He informed me that the carpet layer never, NEVER, under any circumstances, replaced doors.

I asked if maybe the nice, young man with the black hair could do it . . . I wasn't asking for the moon or the King. I just wanted those doors replaced before my husband came home and saw the destruction. They refused . . . soundly! I suppose they were too busy convincing some other silly woman her marriage was going down the drain because she had bare floors.

My husband's attitude was sour. Our marriage was really getting shaky now, and I had w-w carpeting. He worked until past midnight peeling those doors so they would fit. Even if he had wanted to add something gay and flingy to our marriage he couldn't have. He was too tired. By golly, that handsome salesman didn't tell the truth.

As for the Carpet King ... I suppose he has retired by now to his gigantic hen house in the hills. I hope all his carpets have beetles!

POLITENESS PAYS OFF — WITH PLANTS!!

We have a weekend guest. Her name is Phyllis. She's a plant. She is a philodendron. She seems to be pleased to be here.

During a roundtable dinner discussion, one of the younger children raised the question concerning how I knew the plant was a "she" and couldn't it just as well be a Phil instead of a Phyllis. It was obvious that each member of the family was hanging on to my every word, hoping that mother would lunge off into a lurid tale concerning the sex life of the philodendron. My husband just sat there and grinned. He knew I didn't know anything about the sex life of a philodendron.

"A mother just knows!" I told them, pursing my mouth in a prim line which means "Now shut up and eat!" After all, despite the varied hair lengths and the fact every one of them wears blue jeans and flannel shirts, I have been able to sort out my own girls from the boys ... why should a plant be different.

To be quite truthful about this whole thing, I have never been particularly fond of plants. After all, why should I. The minute I bring them in the house they die. This is the reason why I have classified Phyllis as a weekender. I don't want to become too attached. I don't want to get used to seeing her stretching toward the sun, looking cheerful and green and sweet and then some morning come down into the kitchen and find that she's disappeared into the potting soil ... never to grow again. It's too hard on me. It's pretty hard on the plant too.

But Phyllis looks sturdy and she certainly was cheap. I have strong hopes that everything will work out for her. She's a fat, strong looking little thing and only cost 49 cents. I've always felt money isn't everything. Besides I wasn't going to spend $1.99 on something that most likely was going to turn yellow and wither the minute I laid my hands on it. Of course, I haven't told Phyllis this.

16

I have no idea what other people do with their plants but I have a positive attitude about Phyllis. I intend to coax and whisper her into growing up to be a thing of beauty . . . no bug bites, no white edges, no droops and with a strapping, smooth and stalwart stalk. And it certainly won't hurt my family to co-operate. Two or three are most willing to tell her good-morning and ask occasionally, during the day, if she's feeling well and if the window sill is comfortable. The others are protesting that I'm out of my gourd.

But I have very good reasons to be concerned and to reach for what some people might consider extremes. You see, I've tried plant foods, reading thick books, watering twice a day, not watering at all, the sunny side of the window, the shady side of the window and buying artificial plants.

Nothing has worked yet. Why wouldn't treating a plant like a legitimate member of the family pay off?

"If you yell at good old Phyllis like you do me, Mom, she'll die of shock!" one of the boys said, tweaking Phyllis's leaf as he passed.

"If Phyllis puts her dirty socks on the dining room table, she'll get yelled at," I answered. Plant or no plant . . . enough is enough.

But Phyllis has been a good influence. I swear she has. I even lowered my voice when I stepped in the cat's dish. The cat, remembering old times, ran under the bed but Phyllis didn't twitch a root.

And instead of screaming "WILL SOMEONE EMPTY THIS GARBAGE!" I grab a passer-by by the collar, point at the garbage corner and bare my teeth. Once I grabbed my husband by mistake and I thought maybe then, just maybe, Phyllis would hear some things that would shorten her life in a hurry. But he was considerate and didn't even slam the door when he took the garbage out.

I've noticed, too, that now when the kids fight at breakfast they just hit each other instead of flinging loud verbal abuses like before and the stereo is muted and even the automatic ice maker drops its ice quietly. And Phyllis looks good. I'm almost certain I saw her dip her leaf this morning when I got up 15 minutes late and couldn't find the cord to the coffee pot. Rather than lose my temper and throw things like I might have done before she took up residence in my window, I just sat down and sobbed silently.

If Phyllis turns out like I hope she does, I'm thinking of scattering plants in every room in the house.

A SPECIAL TREAT FOR MOTHER'S DAY!

Lives there a mother in this wide, wide world who has not been jolted out of a sound sleep on Mother's Day with the announcement. . .

"Wake up! Wake up! We have your breakfast, Mommy! Happy Mother's Day!"

It is 5:30 a.m. The sun hasn't even gotten up yet. It has another hour to sleep behind the horizon. Lucky sun!

I do not open my eyes. I smell burnt toast and hear a god-awful chest-clutching breathing in my left ear. The breath on my cheek is very moist.

"Good Heavens," I panic! "One of the children must have caught pneumonia during the night. What if they die on Mother's Day!"

I open one eye.

Augie-Doggie is looking down the front of my nightgown.

"Clown!" I murmur, grasping the blanket to my bosom.

I open the other eye. Standing before me are our seven children. I immediately notice that our oldest son is getting taller. I also notice that his hands and feet are turning a light purple from poor circulation. He has either put on his two-year-old sister's pajamas or outgrown his own overnight.

"Look!" one of the children shouts. "We have your breakfast on a tray."

"Wouldn't supper be better?" I ask weakly. "We can all sleep until late afternoon and have an early supper. Doesn't that sound like fun?"

I tried to clap my hands in enthusiasm but my arms were heavy from sleep. I could not raise them from the bed side.

"But it is all done!" a child wailed. (I think it was the purple one.) "I made the eggs and everything."

"Did you wash your hands?" I ask.

A quick glimpse showed me that he had not washed his hands. In fact, he had probably never washed his hands . . . in his life.

But it was Mother's Day. What the heck.

I looked over at my husband. He was very relaxed and very innocent, snoring peacefully and with great grace. He was smiling. I wondered what he was dreaming. I was almost positive he was not dreaming about being awakened at 5:30 on a Sunday morning.

"Wake up! Wake up!" I called to him. "The children have your breakfast! It is Mother's Day!"

Somehow the day was looking brighter already. I sent Augie-Doggie over to his side of the bed to breathe.

"But we didn't make Daddy's breakfast. It is not Father's Day."

"We'll share," I said firmly — and tried again. My husband

sleeps soundly. On all days. It does not have to be a special holiday or Sunday or even Mother's Day or anything like that.

I shook his shoulder and called into his ear . . . "BREAKFAST! LET'S EAT!"

"I AM NOT HUNGRY!" he said, sticking the pillow firmly between his ears . . . and over his ears.

"BUT YOU HAVE TO EAT!" I cried, forcing the pillow from his head. In softer tones I added . . . "It is Mother's Day." After all, I didn't become a celebrant of this particular day all by myself. I did have some assistance. After all!

The shine in his eyes when they popped open was not a happy shine. He looked rather desperate. He looked even more desperate when he saw our breakfast . . .

Rich, black toast was perched on the side of the plate — a lot of rich, black toast. Propped limply in the middle were three soft-curdled eggs, their middles giving off the distinct odor of being saturated with salt and soil. A dab of cereal that no longer had any snap, crackle and pop nestled in the center and a luke-warm cup of last night's coffee stood solidly nearby. And there was a card . . .

"WE LOVE YOU, MOM.
WE REALLY DO!"

Suddenly the toast turned a creamy, golden brown with just enough evenly spread and glistening butter; the eggs had turned a sanitary white and pure yellow, sprinkled with the right amount of salt and pepper; the cereal began a fanfare of snaps, crackles and pops — oh, how melodious — and the coffee was so hot and so fresh I could hardly put the cup to my mouth. It was a beautiful breakfast. It was a beautiful day.

I glanced at my husband. The sleep had disappeared from his eyes and he was as slim and as handsome as the day I married him. The stretch marks vanished from my hips and my double-chins smoothed into one solid, graceful line.

It was Mother's Day, by golly, and no one . . . anywhere . . . had a better right to celebrate than I did. And I was proud. I still am.

Thank you, God. You too, Husband. We did a GOOD job, didn't we?

OF MICE AND COURAGEOUS WOMEN

I cannot imagine living in contentment and tranquility with a mouse in the house. If I did not KNOW there was a mouse in the house, I suppose I could fake it. But at the first rustle in the garbage can I panic.

"Get your gun!" I scream at my husband. "I hear a mouse!"

"Get the cat!" he answers in an uninterested and placid manner as he stretches his legs before the TV.

How anyone can concentrate on Kojak while we are being attacked by mice is beyond me. Besides, he knows full well the cats are fizzles when it comes to catching mice.

I had high hopes for them when they appeared on the home scene as kittens. One came from a family with banking connections. You'd think just the environmental background alone would give it finesse. It has impeccable manners and walks with a dignified paw. But, unfortunately, it prefers left-over rice krispies and jelly beans to the real thing. It feels about eating mice like I do about liver. Zero.

As for the other one, true, its background is a bit shady and parental connections questionable, but I always thought this type of "cat-on-the-street-corner" seasoning was supposed to make it tough and fiery-tempered. Instead a daddy-longlegs crossing its path puts it in a semi-comatose condition for days. I'd hate to imagine what a mouse would do.

So, here I am, with a husband who can live comfortably with scampering little feet and two "chicken" cats. I just wish I could persuade them all that my spending a good portion of each day sitting on top of the refrigerator can be a bore. I do not sit on top of the refrigerator, amid the dust and old grocery circulars, because I think it is a high type of entertainment. I sit up there because I am afraid and do not believe that mice can climb porcelain.

There is very little a well-rounded and intelligent person can do while sitting 5½ feet in the air. The fact that I am well-rounded adds to the fun of my family when I see a mouse and head for higher ground.

"Look at mom go!" yells our son as I dash through the kitchen shrieking, "Help me, help me!" My pulse rate races to a quick 7,350 rpm's ... (or whatever pulse rates come in) ... and it certainly can't be good for someone of my age, whose usual excitement level reaches a pulse rate of minus 10, to become that overheated. Physically and mentally, it can become a drain.

"How can you be so afraid of a tiny, little mouse?" my husband asks. "You have to outweigh it by at least ???? pounds. It's sort of like pitting an elephant against a gnat. Seems to me you have a distinct advantage."

I suppose I would have if I wanted to challenge the mouse to a wrestling match, but I have no intentions of getting that close to one. Besides, who asked him? Anyone who can watch 35 football games a week can't be classified as sensitive anyway. He doesn't understand my mouse philosophy at all.

I can definitely hold my own with door-to-door salesmen, telephone solicitors, the TV repairman, newspaper editors and committee chairmen, but these are things I can see! Tell me, how can you fight something that scuttles around, under your washing machine, and just whips out for a few seconds to see if you are still there and screaming?

According to my mother, having mice was the next thing to a social disease. Nice people didn't have them. And if they did, they didn't admit it to the whole world. However, in a few whispered conversations lately with close-mouthed friends I have discovered that we are not alone in our affliction. Other people have mice too! And they are perfectly respectable people. The females of the family feel just as I do . . . at the first sign of a gray tail . . . it's WAR!

I can't imagine why any self-respecting mouse would want to live here anyway. It's too noisy. He must be off his squeaker. The food certainly isn't all that great, there are no beds left empty in any of the bedrooms. I don't dust a lot and the only real excitement occurs when I can't find my scissors.

You'd think they'd seek out a place where they could live graciously. Like a motel. Where there's room service and someone makes your bed every morning and you don't have to do dishes and music is piped in your room and you can sleep late. Boy, if I were a mouse that's where I'd live.

I'd sure think twice about living in a house where they were trying to kill me. But then maybe mice like to live dangerously. I wonder if they know how they split my serenity. And confuse my life. For example our last attack went something like this . . .

Armed with three mouse traps, some steel wool, a package of D-con, a pound of cheese and a bottle of Excedrin I braved the check-out line at the grocery store. It was obvious that I was not buying supplies for a bridge party.

Of course, I can not set the traps. In fact, I can not even take them out of the grocery sack. I do not even want to touch them. This is where a brave husband comes in handy. I have a friend who is as afraid of mice as I am. So is her husband. They spend a lot of time together on top of the refrigerator. Which is not all bad when you stop to think about it. However, my friend tells me it is not all roses up there. She says romance is definitely cooled when you are terrified.

At our house the tension is thick as the trap is placed behind the garbage can in the kitchen and the clothes hamper in the bathroom. I am all alone . . . alone and waiting for the first snap! When it comes I jump on top of the table. The second snap vibrates through the house. It sounds like a Mafia attack. Machine gun staccato.

"Oh Lord, please make them be empty," I pray as I go to

check the traps. As much as I hate mice I am not ready for the kill. Nevertheless, I have to make dinner and who can cook when just around the corner lies the body (or bodies) of your murder victim.

The traps are not empty. One has been had . . . the other is on the last bead of its rosary. This is too much for me. I go into the living room, cover my head with a pillow and wait until someone comes home from school. A brave someone. A brave someone who eats in the school cafeteria, rides the school bus and once in a while attends teenage dances. Surely, someone who can do all of that and survive won't be afraid of a little, dead mouse. They are! But I am still the mother. Besides, I'm bigger and I promise that together we will get the mouse out.

"I'll just sit here on the couch and help you," I pledge.

"But mother," the child answers. "I can't hear what you are saying with the pillow over your head." Next to mice, I despise a smart-aleck.

We find a pair of heavy, leather gloves and an old cookie tin. The child puts on the gloves and quickly scoops trap and all into the tin. Whap goes the lid and out goes the mouse. The first crisis is past.

Then we begin to think about the mice in the cookie tin. Poor little thing. That's no way to go. It's certainly not very dignified. Buried in a cookie tin indeed.

We find a bit of cotton, a small white box and some of last year's Christmas stickers. This is not going to be a somber burial. Mouse or not, I respect ritual. A hole is dug, the last fall flowers gathered, the cats show up for the funeral and together, the little children, the cats and I bury the mice. It is almost sad.

We're not setting any more traps. It is too traumatic. And as I've said, I haven't seen any mice lately. We've reached a new understanding. I think they are through here. But you and I both know they have all gone somewhere else.

If I were you, I'd go look behind my refrigerator . . . right now!

LET IT SNOW, LET IT SNOW

Well, it happened again last week. It snowed. There's nothing that makes my morning like hearing the radio announcer casually read off the list of school closings on the day of a snow storm. He's so darn bright and cheerful about it. The least he could do is sob a little in between. He must have something against mothers. What's it to him anyway? He's all safe and snug — holed up in his quiet, peaceful little cubbyhole — with nothing to disturb his day but a radio wave. Doesn't he know that he holds the nerve strings of mothers all over the area in his hands.

His most devoted fans are the children in our house. They hang on to his every word. Cheering him on. They were psyched up about 5 a.m., waiting . . . just waiting for the big announcement. On normal days we can hardly move them from their beds 10 minutes before the bus is due. But let the first flake of snow drift to the ground and they become different people.

"Stop dancing around the kitchen," I cried, hunching over my sixth cup of coffee. "It's going to be a long day."

"It's going to be a beautiful day!" sang out one of my loved ones. "Just look at all that gorgeous snow falling and blocking the roads."

"The visibility is practically zero," thrilled another, clapping her hands. "Isn't that groovy!"

"You bet groovy," I growled, popping two aspirin in my mouth. I didn't really need them. My eyes were already as round as a sunburst with all that coffee, but I decided I could use all the help I could get. Things were rapidly going downhill.

But along about 8:45 even their enthusiasm began to wane. Everyone has outgrown Capt. Kangaroo (except me), they've had at least three meals and no one can find anything new in the refrigerator to eat except the "same old things," supposedly they've played every one of the million dollars worth of games they received for Christmas at least three times, the dog has decided to take his chances in the blizzard and begged to be let out and I've taken to carrying the aspirin bottle around in my pocket. Suddenly, the whole house is deathly still! I panic!

"What are you doing?" I scream.

"Nothing."

"Well, quit it!" I know when something rotten is going on. A mother has instincts.

I am determined to be cheerful. I've read about cheerful mothers in books and seen them on television. Besides, I have nothing better to do . . . with the blizzard and all. I decide to try it.

"Let's all clean our rooms," I sing out happily . . . clapping my hands with what I hope is an inspirational and lighthearted clap.

"Icck!"

"Who wants to wash walls?" I smile.

"Double Icck!!"

"I know," I warble gaily. "Let's make snow ice cream."

"The dog's been outside," someone groaned. I had forgotten that.

By now it is about 9:45 a.m. and the whole day stretches ahead like a shroud. I threaten to destroy the TV Guide if one more person complains that they have nothing to do.

Suddenly, the whole house seems to light up with electricity. Bodies scurry off in every direction. Activity reaches a tremendous momentum. They have found something to do. I wonder what it is! I suspect terrible things. They look far too smug. I take a tight hold on my aspirin bottle. I peek into the room.

Some of the children are sitting quietly on the floor listening attentively as another has assumed a strong, authoritative voice and says . . .

"O.K., I'm the teacher and you're the kids . . . your assignment is . . ."

I smile to myself, put the aspirin bottle back on the shelf, let the dog back in and pour another cup of coffee. The day has been saved.

School has opened after all.

COLOR ME CLOTHES

I have been cleaning children's rooms for more than 25 years. This is a job that has no retirement security, no fringe benefits, no available franchises,no chance for advancement, no liberal insurance and no vacations. The only thing I get is a coffee break and I'm usually too nauseated to take advantage of it. Nor can I afford it.

Don't get me wrong — I'm not the "Happy Homemaker" type that runs into their children's rooms each morning with a feather duster, can of spray wax and a smile. I seldom enter the area voluntarily. It usually takes an emergency situation to get me into their rooms — an emergency situation like fear for my life.

"The whole top floor is going to decompose if they don't clean their rooms," I warn my husband. "Mark my words. The floor will just rot away and fall on our heads some night as we sleep."

"You are over-reacting again," he said. "It can't be that bad."

He has untold faith in his children . . . and trust . . . and confidence. And he is blind. And his sense of smell has faded.

"Well, it is!" I told him. "And someday I'll have a stroke when I go up there. You wait and see. Then you'll all be sorry."

He didn't seem too worried, even though he knows that I become quite upset (perhaps deranged is a better word) when I do decide to clean the children's rooms.

It is an all-day affair. It is a day that I put the crock-pot to work, do not answer the telephone, dress in throw-away clothes and use all the plastic garbage bags. It is a Project. A Project I have never seen covered in a woman's magazine.

Magazine articles are filled with helpful hints and advice on jogging for health and beauty; how to adjust to sex in three minutes; casseroles your family will flip over; how to crochet wallpaper in just one weekend and 17 ways to get houseplants to talk back. Not once have I ever read how to keep a dresser drawer from becoming gangrenous or methods of keeping a bed from shriveling or avoiding spoilage in the closet or mold in the makeup box or what to do with dirty magazines found under your son's mattress.

That last one threw me for awhile. I couldn't find anyone to help me with that problem. I just solved it myself in a hurry. I will tell you how. You won't read it in a magazine either.

One of our sons actually is fairly neat. He keeps his things pretty much in order. I don't have to enter his room with a pick and shovel, just a dust rag and clean sheets. And once in awhile I turn his mattress so there won't be any Augie-Doggie body sags in the middle.

"Won't he be surprised," I said to the wall, and I heaved his mattress over, "when he finds a straight, firm mattress to sleep on!"

Guess who got the surprise! Tucked tidily under the mattress, squashed in all their bare-skinned beauty, was a selection of what is known in the Navy and everywhere else I suppose as "girlie" magazines.

"Oh, my goodness," I said, out loud . . . to the wall. "Oh, my goodness!" I had grown up in a household where True Story was banned. This discovery was almost too much for my nervous system. I nearly had the stroke I had been promising.

Thumbing through one of the magazines, my eyes became round and quite large.

"Well, I never," I said.

Sorting underwear became pretty tame all of a sudden. I certainly didn't know what to do with those magazines. My husband wasn't home. I couldn't ask his advice. I didn't want to, anyway. I didn't think he should see those pictures. I wasn't going to take a chance that HE might have a stroke.

Throwing them in the garbage was not the answer. I knew that. There was this chance the garbage men might have weak hearts and I didn't want that hanging over my head. Suddenly I knew just what to do . . call it mother's instinct. Finding a box of crayons, I methodically and painstakingly colored clothes on every one of those ladies — with great style, too, I might add. Dior couldn't have done any better. With tenderness I put them back under the mattress.

"There now, girlies," I said. "You'll be much warmer with clothes on."

I was satisfied. I had done a good day's work.

That evening while we were having dinner my husband asked his usual end-of-the-day, original, stimulating conversational question . . . "And what did you do exciting today?"

"Oh, I colored!" I answered.

Heads all around the table came up. They hadn't heard that before. I smiled smugly. And kept my mouth shut. Only one head kept eating . . . eating a lot. Spinach just flew down his throat. He was eating it right out of the serving dish, spoonful after spoonful.

And do you know what . . . this boy doesn't even like spinach. Now, what do you think of that?

CROWDING UNDER THE COVERS

Over the years our family has worn out three cribs, two sets of bunk beds, a canopy, a three-in-one trundle and a number of doubles, singles and twins — not to mention a studio couch or two.

Don't get me wrong. These were not worn out by the wear and tear of someone sleeping in them. They were worn out during the process of our very own family game called — "Bed-Basket Turn Over," or more simply, "Everybody Change Beds In The Middle of The Night."

My husband and I did not play this game with willing enthusiasm. Quite frankly we were content to stay just where we originally laid our heads upon retiring. We liked our bed. It was large, soft, yet firm enough and comfortable for just the two of us. However, it was not designed as a "community" bed. In fact, the manufacturer's description of our bed promised that this particular style once graced the bedchambers of pampered French royalty. I was impressed.

"My goodness," I said, "can you imagine . . . sleeping like French royalty?"

"Yeah!" my husband leered.

But I bet one thing — I bet the French didn't intend for nine people and a large, hairy dog to crawl in under their royal covers. Neither did I. You certainly can't be considered pampered when you are squashed in next to the wall.

I had great expectations when our children were small. I really and truly thought they would all appreciate a bed of their own. Actually, I didn't mind that they shared the bathtub, school socks, mittens, training pants, french fries, record players, kittens or even toothbrushes. I did, however, insist they have their own beds.

"Just because we have a large family," I explained to my husband, "does not mean we can skimp on sheets." I didn't want people feeling sorry for our children.

It has turned out that the only people who could go out into the neighborhood and ask for sympathy were my husband and I. It was years before we slept in our bed without uninvited drop-in company after midnight. From the time our oldest daughter learned to climb over the siderails of her crib we had a steady marching of little feet into our bedroom. And the major attack never came until we were fast asleep.

"I'm scared," the first would say. "Can I sleep with you?"

You cannot turn away a frightened child I told my husband. Dr. Spock will get you if you do. So, we took the first one into bed custody. She would get her security sleep.

"I'm cold!" said the second. "Can I sleep with you?" A blue nose appears at my side of the bed. I don't know why they always came to MY side of the bed.

"Your sister's in here," I whispered. "There is no room. Go sleep with your brother."

"I can't. Augie is sleeping with him. He stinks."

"Oh, for goodness sakes," my husband moaned. "I'll sleep in your bed. You sleep here."

"You can't sleep in my bed, Daddy, it's wet."

"I'll scoot over . . . get in." I wanted no potty-training lectures at 2 a.m. So, now we are four. One is slightly damp. It is crowding up.

It is not long before Nos. 3, 4 and 5 turn up. They have their reasons . . . "Augie is snoring and I can't sleep" . . . "The curtains are blowing and I think they are ghosts" . . . and "I heard all of this running around . . . has Santa Claus been here?" In unison . . . just as if they have practiced . . . they chorus . . . "Can I sleep with you?"

"Do you think," my husband asked in a low and trembling voice, "if I snore and stink I could manage a night's rest? I'll go sleep in the scary room. I am not afraid of curtains."

He leaves. I really do not expect to see him again until breakfast. One thing about him . . . he doesn't hop in and out of beds. Well, at least I don't think he does. But we won't go into that. At least not right now.

At this particular moment — in our lovely French-styled bed — I am sleeping with five children and a hairy dog who evidently was frightened when the cat crawled in bed with him. Augie spread across my feet. I do not feel one bit pampered.

And I cannot sleep. The children and Augie are asleep. I am clinging to the side of the bed, my pillow is gone and I have no blanket. Only my feet are asleep. Quietly and with great stealth I left the room to search for a bed. Automatically, I eliminated the damp bed, the one with the cat and the crib. Nor did I want to take a chance on running into Santa Claus in September. I could not afford him. This leaves a top bunk with ghostly curtains. It is occupied but I know the occupant well.

"Move over," I hissed to my husband. "I'm going to sleep with you!"

"Good grief," he answered.

That shot my theory about our being royalty — bed or no bed. I certainly can't imagine any red-blooded Frenchman reacting like that . . . can you?

SCHOOL BUS VIRUS

We have discovered a miraculous cure for the common cold at our house. There is a strong possibility that it will make the medical journals, side-by-side with brain transplants or something equally fantastic. It is called "Instant Recovery As Soon As the School Bus Is Out Of Sight!"

Picture the child who comes down the stairs, gasping with lung congestion and bent double with paroxysms of chilling coughs. Red eyes, sniffling nose, laryngitis . . . even their hair strings. They look awful.

I am immediately concerned. I promise to call the doctor at the first decent moment and dispense home remedies. Their father and I talk in soft, sympathetic voices and they are allowed to skip oatmeal.

Others in the family, who are expected to go to school and who have not been quite so swift of mind and body, are jealous. They try hard to round up a cough or a sniff and go so far as to pretend fainting in front of me. But they just can't make it. They didn't plan ahead.

From the highly coveted throne on the living room couch, in front of the television and near the candy dish, sick child looks wan and pathetic and gives each brother and sister a parting shot as they go out the door to the bus. The voice is weak and longing . . . "I wish I was going to school today — we're having liver and onions for lunch." It's sort of like a scene out of "Love Story."

The school bus pulls out of the driveway. Little dull eyes follow its progress down the road. It can no longer be seen. Eureka!

The body, which an instant before was racked with a 105-degree temperature, is playing tag with the cat behind the couch. Coloring books, paints, Johnny West and Barbie appear from nowhere on the living room carpet. The TV automatically snaps on and the stereo blares. Magically the appetite returns and peanut butter and jelly sandwiches dance in single file out of the kitchen. Followed by Kool-aid.

The whole room glows with health. The Vicks bottle has rolled under the couch, the thermometer droops in the ashtray and the kleenex box, which before had been dispensing tissues like a computer, lies neglected.

Once, just for fun, I yell "Look! Look! The school bus has turned back. It is coming this way!" Sick child, bombing around vigorously, suddenly turns weak and drops into horrible chills and tries desperately to break out in a rash.

"Gotcha!" I say. Sick child has been had. We go back to school at noon. We enter the building hand in hand . . . I was taking no chance there would be a break for it at the last minute. The wafting smell of liver and onions rolls down the hallway. Mother smiles in deep satisfaction.

Sick child is just in time for lunch.

VACATIONS ARE FOR CHIPMUNKS

We have spent the past month or two trying to decide where to go on vacation. I rather wanted to go somewhere near a city where we could stay in an expensive hotel, take in a few Broadway shows, eat gourmet meals and use our credit cards at exclusive boutiques.

The children wanted to go to a rock festival.

My husband said, "Wouldn't it be fine if we could go where the streams run clear, the trees grow tall and the air is cool and sweet?"

I reminded him that this type of atmosphere often included things like wolves and large snakes.

"I don't think so," he said. "Besides wolves and large snakes are not much more dangerous than city traffic and the things that go on at rock concerts."

I could see the reflection of rainbow trout in his eyes.

He's the one, in fact, who dragged us all to Canada a few years ago.

I had no objections to going to Canada. This gave the children a chance to fight on foreign soil and to discover that restrooms and pop machines are all the same... Canadian and American. This seemed to be the most important discovery they made during the entire vacation.

However, I am a firm believer that vacation spots should be chosen for their proximity to home — like 15 minutes from takeoff to arrival. Traveling in a car for hundreds of miles with seven children who can hardly tolerate the sight of each other under the best of circumstances, such as separate bedrooms and unlimited use of the telephone, is not my idea of domestic, family relaxation.

During the two or three days it took us to reach our vacation spot in the land of Canadian sky blue waters and giant mosquitoes I often compared traveling with our children to that of inviting a group of grizzly bears to share our car.

"Don't forget Mama Bear!" my husband grinned. Granted, my disposition was not always sunny, but when your sole responsibility is to see that 3,000 facial tissues don't escape and cover the driver's eyes while the car is racing down the interstate; to limit the occupancy of the front seat to four (the rear of the station wagon remains empty); to supervise the water jug and glide through fascinating countryside sloshing ankle deep in icy water while the air conditioner vent blows cold gusts on your feet . . .

To explain 130 times why it is virtually impossible to install innerspring mattresses in cars for sleeping comfort; to keep the boys from Indian wrestling over the stomach of the little sister who has a tendancy for car sickness; to modify and tone down their father's answer when the four oldest ask for T-bones for supper and to watch for a smiling lady riding a red bicycle and tipping off the littlest child so she can finally win in car bingo and quit sobbing — none of this brings on cheery smiles and hearty chuckles from the lady in the front seat.

Especially from a lady who was tired of vacations. Already. And ours hadn't even started.

We had rented a cabin by a lake. It had hot and cold running chipmunks.

After arrival the children were on a tear for 30 minutes. Swim, change clothes, fish, change clothes, a trip to see the lodge, change clothes, out in the boat, change clothes, drink two cans of pop, change clothes, eat three candy bars and write five postcards back home, change clothes, a quick game of jarts, croquet, lawn tennis and minature golf and change clothes. In a half an hour they had wiped out their vacation and entire wardrobe.

"There's nothing to do," they wailed standing behind their dirty clothes. You could hardly see the whites of their eyes. "And we have nothing to wear!"

"Go sit by the lake and listen to the loons," my husband suggested. He is a hopeless romantic.

"They sound like Augie does when he gets his tail caught in the screen door," one of the boys said. So much for the loons.

Crossing over the Canadian border was exciting. I had never been out of the United States. The people at the border were friendly, polite and gracious. They welcomed us with opened arms. Getting out was a different story but I'll go into that later.

It was obvious to the native Canadians that we were tourists. We had on all the wrong clothes. Granted, they were clean, for I was spending four hours a day in the laundromat, but they were all wrong. Thinking of a late Nebraska summer I did not take into consideration that during our visit to Canada the sun would hardly shine and that nor'easters and near blizzard conditions would exist while we were there.

I went up and down streets taking pictures. This, of course, pointed the finger at me, labeling me tourist. I didn't care. In truth, the reason I was taking so many pictures was not for scenic value but to keep warm. The flash bulb warmed me for a one split-second. That was better than nothing.

And I didn't sleep much nights. I could hear wolves. I truly could. My husband told me it was traffic from the highway wafting over the lake but, by golly, I knew better. I knew there were wolves out there — the brochures said so — and I did not intend to be a five-course dinner while I was asleep.

Our cabin had three bedrooms, a living room, kitchen and bath. The lock on the door was sturdy. I wiggled it everytime I went by, just to be sure.

We visited royal gardens, shopped unique little stores, explores museums, went fishing and swimming in the cold, clear lakes, hiked beautiful, tree-lined trails and sat in the Canadian moonlight after the children went to bed.

We picked out-of-the way grocery stores for shopping. The shelves were stocked with goods labeled in French. I used my high school French to decipher the necessary grocery items we needed. Some we could recognize by trademarks. The rest I chose with my knowledge of the language. I made a few mistakes. Everyone is entitled to one or two and I admit I felt rather foolish when I opened a can of bathroom cleanser when I was mixing baking soda biscuits. It took a while for me to convince my family I certainly had not flunked French.

When it came time to leave none of us wanted to go. We practically considered ourselves subjects and I was thinking of learning to curtsy properly in case we ran into the queen.

When we approached the border to the United States we discovered they checked cars. Before they had just saluted and waved us on through. We stopped in line while the two cars ahead of us were thoroughly searched and inspected. Packages were removed and occupants were taken into the customs station. We watched all of this in awe.

"What if they don't let us go home," I whispered to my husband. The Star Spangled Banner ran through my head. All of a sudden I wanted to save my citizenship — and that of my family.

"Good heavens," he answered, "don't get excited. We don't have anything to hide. People go through here every day without trouble."

I wasn't so sure. The people ahead of us were still in the customs office and they certainly looked innocent enough.

By the time the inspector reached our car I was wrought with guilt. My face, blue-gray from two weeks of cold weather, was edged in white. I was scared to death. I knew we had no contraband stashed in the back of the station wagon, no heroin taped under the engine, no hamburger in my purse and we hadn't even spent much money. Nevertheless, my whole body screamed "Arrest this woman!!" The little children were huddled in the back seat — even the teenagers were subdued.

The polite officer directed his questioning to me. "Of what country are you a citizen, ma'am?" God, I couldn't remember. Someone in the back seat hissed, "The United States."

That seemed like a reasonable answer, so I gave it. The officer seemed satisfied.

When he asked about carrying plants or growing things of that nature, I shoved a loaf of rye bread covered with sesame seeds in his face. I threw in the can of bathroom cleanser for good. He wouldn't even look at that — just glanced with pity at my husband, who was enjoying the whole process. I rather resented his attitude — also my husband's.

The officer's final inquiry was in reference to the children in the back who were all squished together and fighting the fear their dumb mother was going to say something wrong and get us all exiled forever in a foreign country.

"Are the seven children all yours?" he asked with a bored attitude.

By now he knew we were too scared to smuggle. And that's where I blew it.

I should have said, "Seven!! There shouldn't be seven children back there," and gotten rid of the ones who complained the most, pinched the most and had to stop at the bathroom the most.

CONVERSATION WITH CUPID

"Hello, Cupid. I have a bone to pick with you."

"Hi there, dearie. You look a little older than you did last time I saw you."

"Well, I imagine I do. Heavens, that's been a long time ago. What did you expect?"

"Not this!"

"So, I've gained a few pounds. You haven't slimmed down a whole lot yourself. I see you are still toting around that silly bow and arrow. Seems to me you could update your equipment. And get some clothes on."

"Why should I? It works just the way it is."

"It works all right. That's what I wanted to see you about. Personally, I think when you go around twanging people the least you could do is warn them."

"Warn them about what?"

"Well, you know!!"

"No, I don't know and you'd better hurry up and tell me. I have work to do. A lot of work. June will be here before you can say "wedding" and there are still quite a few carefree bachelors out there . . . whisking around in snappy sport cars, with bundles of money, new leisure suits, tennis racquets, expecting a summer of unencumbered golfing, fishing and nights out with the boys. I have my work cut out for me. You, of all people, should see that. You hung around long enough before I got around to you. Why, I remember your husband, by golly he..."

"Which reminds me. He would like to speak to you when I get through. He mentioned just the other night when he was making out our joint income tax return with all those complicated deductions that he'd sure like to get ahold of that stupid Cupid — just once. I certainly can't see what HE has to complain about."

"Think about it!"

"I have. That's why I want to talk to you."

"Get with it — this quiver is getting heavy and I'm freezing."

"For one thing... you didn't mention garbage when you were twittering around. Not once did you mention garbage."

"Why should I mention garbage? That's not my job."

"Do you have any idea how much garbage a 25-year-old marriage brings? You never even hinted at soggy egg shells and wet coffee grounds when you fired off those arrows. There's little romance in a garbage can."

"Just a small detail I overlooked. Next complaint."

"Snoring. You didn't tell me he snored."

"So, he snores. You snore."

"I don't snore!"

"You do snore! I've heard!"

"Sit on it, Cupid!"

"Are you finished?"

"Not by a long shot. What about cooking? Do you realize since you flitted into my life I have cooked 27,375 meals, give or take a few?"

"That's not my problem. That's your husband's problem. I suppose that is one of the things HE wants to see me about. Well, I never promised him you could cook. That's for sure."

"That's not nice. You are a cross old thing. You're supposed to be sweet, cuddly and cherub-like."

"Who can be sweet, cuddly and cherub-like when all they hear are complaints, complaints, complaints! I work my fingers to the bone, wear this ridiculous, cold satin bow and still no one appreciates me no matter how hard I try."

"Are you crying?"

"Sniff. Sniff."

"Don't cry! Please, don't cry! I didn't mean to make you cry!"

"Then you aren't mad at me? Even after all these years . . . with the garbage and the snoring and the cooking and all the other stuff?"

"Of course not . . . why little fellow, what would I do without you!"

"I LOVE YOU, CUPID!"
HAPPY VALENTINE'S DAY

METRIC MADNESS STRIKES

Our junior high daughter came home last week and disappeared into the basement. We did not see her for hours. We had to remind her to come up for dinner. She did not even eat sunflower seeds in the living room. I felt something terrible was probably wrong with her — an incurable disease she didn't want us to know about. I was worried. She continued to go to the basement directly after school for about three days. I could stand it no longer.

"Why are you spending so much time in the basement?" I asked.

"I'm making wheels," she said. "It is an experiment for school."

"It sounds as if you are doing all right," I complimented with relief. "I hear lots of noise."

"That's Augie-doggie making the noise," she answered . . . a tiny tear welled up into her eyes. "He's bumping around down there chasing a cricket. I am not doing so well." The tear spilled over onto her cheek.

My husband cannot stand to see any of his children cry. His wife can conduct a seven-day crying jag, complete with wails and whimpers and all he hands me is a handkerchief, but let his children cry and he turns softie. So do I. Sometimes!

He said, "Bring up your wheels. Let me see them."

She did. They looked fine to me. Two circular cardboards were attached to a sawed-off clothes hanger.

"Why, those are nice wheels," I pointed out. "I like them."

"So do I," she said, more tears running down her face. "But they won't go anywhere. And they are supposed to travel five meters!!"

Those meters! They are the reason why I have decided I am far too old for homework. I did fine with Dick, Jane and Sally and their pet dog, Spot. I did not miss a vocabulary list. And math used to be easy. One squirrel plus one squirrel were always two squirrels. No questions. It was the same with elementary biology. One squirrel plus one squirrel were three squirrels. No monkey business — just plain facts.

35

But now they have thrown in the metric system . . . simply, I am sure, to prove that parents are chronic and classic idiots.

"How far is a meter?" I asked.

"About this far," she answered. She gave a vague measurement.

"How many inches?" I really wanted to know. I can understand inches.

No one would tell me.

"For goodness sakes," I screamed. "How can you get anything to travel five meters if you don't know how many inches it is?"

"They don't use inches anymore," my husband said. "Inches are old fashioned." He laughed and left for the basement with our daughter.

I was determined to find out exactly how many inches made a meter. I'd show them. I called a CPA friend. He was not at home. I called the Junior High math teacher. She was not home either. Finally, I called a friend with a smart husband . . . one that occasionally talked to me as if I had a brain. He had gone to the grocery store.

She thought she knew what a meter was. "A meter is less than an inch," she said. "Five meters would be a very short distance."

I was very happy. That meant the wheels would not have to travel very far. I went to the basement to deliver my joyous message. "Your wheels will only have to travel this far," I said happily . . . measuring a minute distance with my thumb and forefinger.

"Oh no, Mom!" our daughter cried. The tears were really rolling now. "Our teacher says it is this far" . . . and she gave me that vague measurement again. My husband concurred. He was still smiling and very smug. And he was not telling me anything.

I went back to the telephone. My friend answered. She admitted she might have been off an inch or two. "I looked it up in the encyclopedia," she said. "A meter is defined as one ten-millionth of the distance of the earth's surface from the pole of the equator" . . . "Why, that crazy teacher," I exploded. "That means those poor wheels will have to go out our door, up the street and around the square about 1,000 times. The cardboard will never last!"

"A meter is equivalent to 39.37 inches," she sighed. "I'll see you Monday night for bridge." And hung up.

I sat down and tried to turn 39.37 inches into meters. It wasn't easy. Finally I had the measurement. It turned out to be exactly the same as our daughter's vague hand-gesturing one. My husband said he knew it all along. But I wasn't speaking to him. I wasn't speaking to our daughter either . . . nor her

36

teacher. I wasn't speaking to anyone. I had spent the entire evening on those meters. Missed "Starsky and Hutch" and everything.

The wheels made it. They went exactly five meters.

Our daughter got an A in wheels.

All I got was a headache and a determination never to get involved in homework again. Ever! Unless it's Dick, Jane and Sally!

WHITE LEGS LOOK FUNNY ON THE BEACH

All over the country outdoor swimming pools are opening for the summer season.

All over our house people are trying to find last year's swimming suits.

"But I know I put it here," our 14-year-old screams.

She is pointing to the dining room table.

Bear in mind, we have had at least four family dinners at this table in the past nine months: Thanksgiving, Christmas, my birthday and a spur-of-the-moment celebration. Possibly they were not memorable . . . but anybody even a 14-year-old — knows you don't eat pumpkin pie surrounded by a bikini.

"Look in the garage," my husband said sheepishly. He did not say this very loud but with a great deal of conviction in his voice. I had the feeling he knew just exactly where her bathing suit was. I also had the feeling he had used it to clean the car engine.

He often does this. I was not surprised. He does not screen his rags. If something lays unclaimed more than 15 minutes, any article of clothing in our house has a good chance of becoming magically rendered useless.

Few satin nightgowns that I know of have had the distinction of ending their lives as a roto-tiller blade wiper. Mine did. It certainly took the romance out of it in a hurry.

Our college son had difficulty finding his suit too, but for a different reason. Oh, he had it put away carefully but it was so tiny it had disappeared in the crack of the dresser drawer. A piece of elastic, delicately covered with a wisp of nylon tricot, does NOT constitute a bathing suit as far as I'm concerned . . . and I told him so. He just laughed.

On the other hand, I had absolutely no trouble finding mine. Alas, something so large is terribly hard to misplace — no matter how hard you try.

Naturally, I had outgrown it — again. I do that every year.

"How can anyone outgrow something as shapeless as my bathing suit?" I said to myself while hopelessly looking in the mirror. There is very little advertising people can come up with concerning the type of suit I buy. The best they can do is "Built for Comfort and Support."

I stopped buying the kind that shows skin a long time ago. Mine are always the total coverup look. If they ever come out with a turtleneck, I want one.

It is probably my imagination and the fact that I am over-sensitive, but I really and truly feel as if every eye on the beach is ogling me as I pick my way across the sand.

I wear a very loose, terry-cloth swim coat, large hat, sun-glasses and tuck my head down so no one will recognize me. But I have never figured out what to do with my legs. They are exceptionally skinny to prop up such tonnage and they are pale . . . very pale. You could, in all probability, without exag-geration, describe them as stark white.

Last year I thought I had it made. I wore pantyhose under my bathing suit. No more white legs, by golly. They were sleek, tan and looked gorgeous. That day I pranced across the sands. "Let them ALL look," I thought to myself.

True, my legs were a little hot. And my knees were perspiring but I felt sensational. I stretched on the sand like a seashell.

Then I went swimming.

The pantyhose suddenly filled up with water and my legs ballooned-dragging me under like a cement block. I though I was going to drown.

"Help me! Help me!" I screamed at my husband. He was giggling so hard he could not move in the water. I certainly couldn't depend on him.

Well, let me tell you . . . I ripped those pantyhose off in a hurry. I could not get underneath to do it properly and neatly without removing my suit. I didn't want to do that and cause a scene (or a tidal wave) so I just tore wherever possible.

When I emerged from the water little tatters of taupe hung from my suit. My feet were enclosed in neat, 20 denier with nude heels. In between my white legs radiated-reflecting off the sand.

There was absolutely no doubt this time; every eye on the beach was turned in my direction.

Some people were very nice — mostly women over 40 wearing comfortable and supportive bathing suits. They turned their heads and pretended to fumble in their thermos bottles or read a book.

Some people were not so nice. One in particular was laughing — very hard.

His face was familiar. I had known him all his life.

He was wearing a wisp of colored nylon.

LIVING WITH THE FAMILY HORSE

Our Pony Purchase anniversary is coming up soon. We don't celebrate much. Oh, we might have shredded wheat for supper and maybe someone will give a nostalgic whinny and my husband and I will bow our heads, briefly, and solemnly swear never to buy another pony — but other than that it will pass rather quietly. You see, we really don't like to stir up the memory.

According to theory, every child wants a pony. I never did but then I was a strange child. I read Black Beauty, all right, and in later years wondered what it would be like to ride into the sunset with Matt Dillon but that's about as far as it went.

But our children wanted a pony. And my husband was convinced we should add to our zesty country living by going ahead with a pony purchase.

"You shouldn't live in the country without a pony," he said. I didn't think we should live in the country with or without a pony but that's another story.

Naturally, the children promised on bended knee that they would feed, water, curry and give TLC to any and all ponies we bought. Their father and I would not have to lift a hand. All we would be required to do was put up the money and watch them ride gracefully by and applaud their horsemanship. One even dreamt of winning blue ribbons at the fair. Parents just can't fight that kind of stuff.

It was an excited group that went to buy the pony. She was a cream-colored Shetland, not too tall and not too fat. She stood there, head bent and hoofs primly placed. She looked easy to get on, not too hungry and very gentle. She looked, in fact, perfect.

I thought it was a little strange that the man we bought her from seemed so over-anxious. He didn't even stroke her mane in farewell, just walked back into his house, laughing and rubbing his hands together as we led her away. But it was a fleeting doubt.

She behaved herself nicely as we tied her to the back of the station wagon and led her home. She trotted along trying not to hang back . . . not wanting to inconvenience us in any manner.

"My goodness," I thought. "What a little lady she is!"

What a fool I was!

The children had worked for a week . . . getting her room in the shed ready. It was cleaner than theirs. They named her "Candy" and established her in her new home with hugs and kisses.

She delicately nibbled her way through the bale of hay we had placed there. My husband's eyes became very wide as the pony looked around for more to eat. She began to gnaw on our eight-year-old daughter. This was our first indication that we might have made a bad purchase.

Two days passed. The pony had eaten everything bought for her. My husband had actually planned that the hay would last through the winter. She had eaten it all in 48 hours. The eight-year-old was terrified and stayed locked in her room every time someone led Candy from the shed. The 10-year-old immediately fell off and broke her arm, missing three days of school.

The 12-year-old claimed the pony "smelled" and that if she went near it she, too, would "smell" and the 14-year-old's feet touched the ground whenever he got on her back.

"I can walk faster than I can ride," he said and went back to the refrigerator.

Candy the Pony stood out in the yard and looked in the kitchen window. She had ticked off the whole family — except one. Guess who that was! We became practically inseparable.

There was little doubt that the pony recognized, at once, that she had met up with a pansy.

Every morning my husband gaily went to work, my children happily went to school and I gritted my teeth and went out to the pony. After all, someone had to tether her outside so she could eat grass. She wasn't getting any more bales of hay...at least, not right away.

And she had to be watered. I hauled gallons of buckets of water to that pony. And she kicked them all over, then stood there with her tongue hanging out...just like she was in the middle of the dessert. Her mane turned dry and dusty. She began to shed. I thought she was going to dry up.

"What AM I going to do?" I asked my husband. "She will dehydrate and die and I will go through life knowing I am a pony-murderer."

"You have to be smarter than the horse," my husband said.

For someone who had just written a $40 check for a two-day supply of hay I wasn't sure he was the one to turn to for advice but I had nowhere else to go.

My knowledge of ponies had been limited to (a) movies; (b) television; (c) books; (d) plastic statutes; (e) the tote board. I did not understand...or even admire...one that reared on its hind legs, pawed the air, rolled its eyes back until the red showed and suggested signs of being convulsive.

"That's a crazy pony!" I told my husband. "I think she's loco!" I had heard that word applied to horses. I supposed it applied to ponies, too. At least it seemed to apply to this one.

Candy had been with us, by now, for two weeks. No one else

in the family even acknowledged she was in the neighborhood if they could help it.

My husband reassured me. "You have a way with animals," he said. "Just be patient and loving . . . you will win her trust and affection."

A lot he knew.

Every day I went to Candy's shed with hope reborn. And every day she curled back her lip and tried to eat my arm off. Every day I tied her to a concrete block to graze and every day she ran away.

It became routine for a kind passer-by to tap on the back door and inquire if the pony trotting down the road lugging the concrete block was ours. I was too honest to say "No" and too polite to tell them to mind their own business . . . so I just stopped answering the door. I practically became a recluse.

It became a before-dinner ritual — just like peeling potatoes — to climb in the car and go out to look for Candy. I made the children go with me. They didn't want to.

"It's your pony," they said with great feeling, actually believing it was true. I soon set them straight on that and insisted they get in the station wagon.

Ideally, and when the day went right and Candy cooperated, our 14-year-old son clutched the rope and Candy trotted steadily along behind. The others watched for traffic. We'd be home in time for me to put the potatoes on. It wouldn't take much more than 15 or 20 minutes out of our day.

This was under ideal conditions, you understand. And it worked for awhile. Then the pony discovered this was pretty dull, routine stuff. She became apprehensive about getting in a rut. And she didn't want to do that. Perish the thought.

One day, Candy made her move. She suddenly picked up her pace and started to gallop down the road. I was doing a swift five miles per hour when I glanced out the side window and saw this cream-colored shetland streak over my left shoulder.

"Speed up! Speed up!" the children shouted. "She's going to pass us!" In fact for a brief moment it looked as if Candy might pull us home this time.

I hit the accelerator. We began to whizz down the country road. The pony's hoofs pounded the gravel, her mane stretched, her eyes rolled back, saliva frothing.

Our son looked as desperate as the pony. His hair was tousled and sticking out, perspiration poured from his face. The only difference was, he wasn't frothing, not yet, anyway. His knuckles were gripped white from holding onto the rope.

Suddenly the pony stopped, dead in her tracks. Our son flew out the rear of the station wagon.

I heard him scream as he flew . . . "You're trying to kill me! Mom! You're trying to kill me!"

41

It wasn't me that was trying to kill him. It was that pony. I tried to explain this to him as I bathed his bruises and picked the gravel from his knees. I'm not sure I convinced him.Our relationship has been strained since.

And then Candy disappeared. We couldn't find her. Even when we drove around and around the sections. She would go away for a few hours and then just as mysteriously pop up again along about dawn.

"Perhaps she has a fellow," my husband grinned. "A little romance never hurt anyone. Not even a pony."

I knew what that meant. At least I thought I knew what that meant — a pregnant pony. Just what I needed. Two ponies for me to care for. Oh boy!

But we were wrong. We soon found out where Candy was really going. A gentleman up the road called and let us know. She was going into his garage and doing all sorts of things. And he did not like it. He told me this in no uncertain terms and with some words I had never heard before and hope to never hear again.

"If you do not come and get this pony," he shouted. "I am going to keep her."

"She's yours!" I answered quickly.

"Well, we've solved that problem," I thought.

We didn't of course.He really didn't want her. He was only kidding. And in further funny words he said so. He mentioned things like sheriffs, lawsuits, and personal property damage.

I gave my family a choice: me or the pony. It took a while but they gave the pony away. I tried not to laugh and rub my hands when the new owners led her away.

I understand she turned into placid, perfect pony — gentle, uncomplaining, hardly eats a thing and is content to stay in the yard without being tied. She's ridden by dozens of children every day. She even smells good.

I don't believe a word of it. But I'm not going to ask any questions. Would you?

A NOT-SO-PRACTICAL CHECK-LIST

Recently I read an article concerning the organization and structured orderliness of getting children off to school in the morning. I am positive it was written by a woman without children, a man who leaves for work at 6 a.m. or someone who is under the heavy influence of tranquilizers. It was definitely not written by anyone I have talked to within the last 25 years.

But because the article sounded so optimistic, claimed the morning rush hour could be turned into a calm, happy adventure for all and because I am sick and tired of wickedness so early in the mornings . . . I decided to adopt the suggested methods.

First of all it said we should all sit down as a happy family group and talk about the problems. This is fine if you can find your family. We didn't all get together until about 11:30 p.m. By then everyone was too tired to consult. Including me. Augie-doggie was the only one who seemed interested. He doesn't have any problems in the early morning. He just doesn't bother to get up. My husband says he is the only smart one in the house.

A suggested check-list went like this: (1) Get Dressed; (2) Comb Hair; (3) Make Bed; (4) Eat Breakfast; (5) Smile. It sounded so simple. I posted the five steps in each bedroom, the bathrooms and the upstairs hallway.

"There," I said with confidence, "now, we will have a peaceful, quiet, systematic approach to this "before school" business. We will no longer act like lunatics in a madhouse but act like a family with class." Previous experience with lists should have alerted me that this one, too, had great chances of failure.

The list had not taken into consideration that in our family one cannot get dressed and comb hair without first washing the body to be dressed and the hair to be combed. Never mind that this had already been done before bedtime . . . and after school and after dinner. Our children are not too keen on homework and doing dishes but they are certainly clean kids — and modest.

They will not share the shower with anyone. And they use a lot of water — mostly hot. The last one in the bathroom can be heard screaming in pain and shivering right through the walls as torrents of icy cold water pelt their body. My husband screams, too, as the water from the upstairs drips down on him as he is shaving.

And the towel situation is really bad. No one has a dry one. They have used a month's supply the day and evening before and have nothing to dry on but kleenex. I keep a towel hidden, I'm O.K.

With wet hair and wet bodies they attempt to get dressed and comb hair. They have no shoes nor do they have a comb. They had them all yesterday. But now they are gone. No one knows where they have gone, least of all me. I know where mine are, I have hidden them.

Now we approach the period where each child accuses the other of being a rotten thief, a nerd and a turkey. The sound level is rising. My husbands clutches a cup of coffee. The china

43

is cracking under the pressure. I am cracking under the pressure. I repeat the mother's old and tired phrase ... "If you had put them away where they belong ... etc., etc., etc." No one pays any attention to me. They continue to call each other thief, nerd and turkey.

We find it is necessary that one child wear pantyhose for "dress-up" day. This was not on the list. She has no pantyhose. At least she cannot find them. They are with her good shoes and comb. I am the only one with pantyhose. They are hidden. The child is sobbing. In the background sisters and brothers are scrambling in happy confusion for the day's supply of socks, sweaters and schoolbooks. Two are wrestling in the hallway. My husband has replaced his china cup with a plastic one. He is shredding his toast nervously. Augie-doggie is snoring in the corner, his head under the couch.

"What is more important," I say to myself, "my stashed supply of pantyhose or my sanity?" I give her my pantyhose. They are Queen size. She is a tubular teen with no hips or thighs. The hose sag over her torn tennis shoes and she sobs louder. With a switch of elastic and three large safety pins I fix them and ease them to fit. She is presentable.

"Don't take P.E. or do anything else," I warn. I wonder how she will make it through the day. In fact, I wonder how I will make it through the day. I'm convinced my husband won't.

We have no time for bedmaking or eating breakfast. We've only accomplished two things on that silly list. And the bus is coming and there is one more thing to do.

As the children chase the school bus down the road I stand in the doorway waving cheerfully and remind them of the final item on the list . . .

"Don't forget to smile!" I shout.

SOMETIMES LITTLE KIDS SWEAR

I know about little children that say naughty words. The first time I heard one of ours come out with a swift swear word I blamed myself.

"Good Heavens," I sobbed to my husband, "I've always kept his pablum warm, his shoes are not hand-me-downs, the nursery rhymes I read him are clean and I watch who he plays with. What happened?"

"Nothing," my husband answered. "He'll be all right. He is not going to juvenile court because he talks dirty. Just watch."

44

I have full confidence in my husband's opinion. I watched. When our son was five I diverted his attention with cookies or building blocks and I never, never left him in a room alone with his grandfather. By the time he was seven he had learned to read and was intermingling four letter words that appear on public buildings with "Jump, Puff, jump."

Fortunately, his teacher was experienced and believed me when I told her he certainly didn't learn THAT word at home. With a brand new teacher, straight out of college, you might have to provide references.

Eventually he was 11 and getting serious — and smart. He started to catch on and pass the buck. I heard things like "Well, Daddy says it," or "Remember when the skillet fell on your foot, Mom, and what YOU said." I used simple psychology. I bribed him . . . and appealed to his sense of independence. I promised him that when he reached the age of 21 he could say and do anything he wanted.

He was so busy making a list of things to do at 21 that he forgot to swear. After I read the list I sort of wished he would go back to the foul language. He included things like staying up all night; NEVER going to school; living in a tent; having 16 dogs and no cats; shooting fireworks every weekend (without supervision); seeing R rated movies; buying a water bed; never changing his underwear; never speaking to his sisters again and living out of reach of his mother. He also listed a few things he had noticed his father doing but we won't go into that.

He changed when he went into junior high. He wasn't saying naughty words. He wasn't saying anything. From a son that I used to hearing prattle night and day, every minute, telling triumphs, hurts and fears he turned into a silent, solemn machine that did nothing but eat. I became complacent. I felt we had turned a big corner.

I was wrong. He had a reputation among his peers. His junior high counselor didn't tell me this. He was too tired. I learned it from the mother of a junior high girl. Girls tell their mothers everything . . . especially about boys. I found out the best thing to do is deny that you have a son in junior high, even if the last name is the same.

I never heard him swear during the senior high age. In fact, I never heard him. He was never home. He had a girl — the same one who used to rat on him in junior high — a girl and a group of friends that looked and acted just like he did. Occasionally this group of friends would bunch up in the front yard while he came in to beg for money. He certainly wasn't swearing then. He was at his charming best, suave, flattering and begging. I couldn't beat the odds.

When he was finally out of high school I gave myself a little lecture. "Now look," I told myself, "you've taken this boy to

45

Sunday school on Sundays, taught him to say "please and thank you," took him to the fire chief when he set the waste basket on fire; served as den mother for three years and saw to it his father had a "talk" with him. (I was never quite sure what they talked about but at least I brought them together). Now he is 'out there.' It is out of your hands."

Actually, swearing was the last thing I had to worry about. Not too long ago, the day came. He was finally over 21. I had dreaded the day for years. As I lit his birthday candles I thought about that list. I could hardly sing "Happy Birthday."

Oddly enough he is still attending college; lives in a house; changes his socks often; wears a necktie when the occasion demands; treats his sisters with respect; has outgrown fireworks completely and thinks they are a waste of money; probably does attend R-rated movies but has the decency not to mention them to me; offered to let his dad and me borrow his water bed . . . and seems to have turned out well despite me.

He was home this past weekend. He offered to mow the lawn. He was so tall, so handsome, so tanned, this son of ours, that I could not resist stepping out on the front walk to watch him.

The mower stopped. He couldn't get it to work. He stood back, gave it a swift kick and said one of his favorite, pre-school words.

He sounded just like his father. I was so proud of him.

BABIES DO GROW UP — DARN IT!

It dawned on me when our oldest daughter celebrated her 16th birthday by asking for . . . and getting . . . a wiglet, bikini underwear and a purse size flask of Chanel No. 5 that things were certainly changing around our house. We had a grown-up daughter.

This was brought to light that same summer when our oldest son burst into our bedroom and announced that the boy who came to pick up his sister had lots of hair on his legs.

Until then her collection had consisted of under-nourished, shorter than she was (and she was barely 5'1") 15-year-olds with razor-like shoulder blades and more ears than physique. This one was on his way to college and flapped his muscles around in a skin-tight melon green bathing suit with a small hand towel wrapped around his neck. Certainly the hand towel was used to keep the hair from tickling his shoulders; it wasn't used to cover up any vital parts, that's for sure.

Out of the corner of my eye I could see my husband bristle
and begin to flex HIS muscles. I didn't know what he had in
mind but I really didn't think he was under the impression he
could actually punch the kid in the nose just because he happened to ask our daughter to the beach.

Just as we grew to like this one and to trust him when they
went out in a car she announced that she couldn't bear the
sight of him for one more minute and brought home a transit in
tight pants with longer hair than mine and granny glasses. I
flexed my muscles at this one and he, too, disappeared somewhere, thank God. Personally, I think he crawled back into the
woodwork. This was my opinion. And then I made my first-of-
many mistakes in dealing with a teen-age child . . . I expressed
my opinion.

"Well, I certainly am glad HE is gone. I didn't think much of
him."

Immediately she broke into her "you-don't-understand, I-am-
grown-up, don't you-trust-me, it-is-all-your-fault" routine. I was
stunned. And surprised. I was new at this business. Perhaps it
was all my fault.

"I'm a bad mother," I sobbed into my husband's neck when
he walked into the door from work.

"They've had a big fight!" offered our son who had watched
the whole thing with big ears and obvious enchantment.

"Everyone has been crying but me," added our four-year-old
who had been busy dismantling the kitchen cupboards while
my attention was diverted. The third-grader was sobbing in the
corner. She didn't have a reason — she just didn't want to pass
up any reason for a good cry. The others, including Augie-
Doggie, were milling around. It was turning into a spectator
sport equal to the Golden Gloves.

My husband calmly removed my nose from his throat and
suggested everyone settle down, pull themselves together, talk
this over quietly and then pointed out that a good, hot meal
might make us all feel better.

This brought on more sobs as I had completely forgotten to
cook anything in the moment of trauma. A failure as a mother
. . . and now a failure as a wife.

Our oldest daughter was dramatically crouched at the
kitchen table, head folded sadly in her hands, mumbling, "No
one ever listens to me. I'm treated like a baby. I am going to
run away."

"I will pack for you," said her sister. "I will help," said her
brother. It sounded like the "Little Red Hen" in reverse.

"I wish I had my own .410 shotgun," threw in our youngest
son. He was only 10 and his hunting experiences were limited
to walking behind his father and carrying the thermos. But he
thought the time was ripe and he might get a "yes" answer in

the confusion. "Jim Adams has his own .410 and new boots, too, and he's three months younger than I am."

"You are much too young," I said quickly. I might have been borderline hysterical but I wasn't stupid. Not yet — anyway — that comes a few years later ... when they all grow up. "You'd kill yourself!"

"Or me!" said my husband hungrily.

Our oldest daughter's problems were fading. She was buffing her nails.

"Jim Adams is rich," said the third-grader, who had stopped sobbing and was making her own dinner of peanut butter spread on banana. "He has his own TV, a new 10-speed bike and gets to buy five comic books a week."

"But look how lonely he must be," I added. Jim Adams was an only child.

Well, that did it. It ended the arguments. Fearing I was going into one of my lengthy and worn around the edges lectures on how lucky they were to be poor and have so many loved ones, they all quietly walked away and left me with their father. He was no fun to lecture ... he was too busy spreading peanut butter on a banana.

I have learned one thing about family fights ... nobody wins. Especially me.

RSVP, PLEASE, MR. CARTER

I have always felt that any type of party I might give is better off catered at eight bucks a head with a professional cleaning organization working like crazy for 30 days prior to it.

Unfortunately, our children have not inherited my hesitant attitude. They will have a party at the drop of a napkin. In fact, I think our youngest daughter was terribly disappointed because President Carter did not accept her invitation to sleep over at our house when he hit the campaign trail in Nebraska.

She had no qualms about asking him to share the guest room with the sewing machine, an old bird cage, a dress dummy, the dog's bed, a box of unmatched socks, my knitting projects, a 16-year supply of magazines, four dead Christmas poinsettias and a couple of bales of macrame rope.

"He wouldn't care, mom," she said.

But I think he would, Don't you? After all, when you shoot for the White House, macrame rope and dead poinsettias are not exactly what you are after in sleeping decor.

That's the way our children are. They've always been this way. Several years ago our two oldest girls planned a surprise anniversary party for us. I think it was our 13th. Behind my back and without my supreme permission they invited 24 adults to our house for a party.

Can you imagine — 24 adults in MY living room looking at MY cobwebs! I don't even have dishes for more than 12.

But these two little girls, with no more experience than a Housekeeping Badge in Girl Scouts, planned, executed and brought forth the whole thing . . . complete with party games, refreshments and conversations which they managed to steer with interesting comments like . . .

"I hope no one minds that the coffee is cold. We didn't know we were supposed to keep the plug in . . ." and

"We dropped all the ice cream in the sink when we were getting it out of the box. But we scooped up most of it before the cat licked it all up . . ." You should have seen the gags go around the room on that one.

I gagged too, when I thought how my reputation as a housekeeper had just gone down the drain . . . a dirty drain in all probability.

Everyone was touched by the thoughtfulness of our children. They said the condition of the house didn't matter. They said they didn't even notice it. I was touched too. I was stabbed.

Their idea of cleaning house is running the floor waxer over the dining room table and folding the evening newspaper. I kept hoping no one stayed around long enough to go into the bathroom. But, of course, they did. And they came out laughing.

That really bothered me. Ordinarily bathrooms are not funny places. They are usually rather dull. You all know that.

I poked my husband. "Maybe you'd better go in there," I said. "Something's going on. You don't think the boy's have written some of those awful things they learned at school on the walls, do you?"

The color drained from my husband's face. "I'll go look," he said.

He came out laughing, too. He had a paper in his hand. It had been posted on the wall.

RULES OF OUR BATHROOM
(please, obey)

1. Last one out of bathtub pull out plug and last one out of bathroom clean up floor.

2. Don't put dirty clothes in the bathroom — put them in the utility room. Our mother gets mad if you get messy.

3. The wastebasket is emptied every Friday. Do not fill it too fast as this is only Sunday and we have a lot of days to go.

49

4. FLUSH TOILET WHEN DONE.
5. Don't take magazines in bathroom.
6. BOYS clean off rim every time you get it all wet because the GIRLS don't like it.
7. Don't leave towels on the floor to be stepped on.
8. Clean off sink.
9. Obey these rules and you will get along fine at our house.
Thank you, please!
I wonder if Jimmy Carter has to put up with things like that in the White House.

SCIENTIFIC PHYSICAL FITNESS

Recently one of our college sons started taking his education seriously. Prior to this he had been devoting much of his time to "learning to live away from home." This took up a lot of his day, leaving little for severe study.

After all, it takes awhile to learn to wear unmatched socks with pride; find a female who is willing to patch and mend; adjust the digestion to unbalanced meals; promote money-making schemes and when they fail, settle for living on 25 cents a week; discover which is stronger — his past upbringing or his present environment and when the past loses, practice blocking a mother's image from his mind . . . a mother's image that shakes her head and waggles her finger.

This all takes time. It is typical. My husband and I understood this. We were willing to wait. We knew that eventually he would figure out why he was there spending all that money at random.

Now we are not so sure we aren't ready for him to return to the confused state of an undeclared major. Now we are not so sure we were right when we gave him the old parental lecture on wasting money without reason. Now we are not so sure that poverty is not preferable to prostration. For you see, he has become a physical education major — a physical education major with a purpose. At this time it seems his main purpose is eliminating his parents.

"OK," he said a few weeks ago when he came home for a visit. "It is time the two of you got in shape."

He was looking right at his dad and me. Both of us are aware that our shapes would not win any prizes but until now we thought we had fooled the children. We thought they thought all parents looked like that. See what a college education will do for you? Destroys images. We didn't know that would happen. We were surprised. We were even more surprised when we found out what he wanted us to do.

"I am going to set up a physical fitness program for you," he went on. "But before I do you must have a complete physical."

"I just had one," I explained. "So did I," my husband added.

Both of us had held our doctor spellbound with our inability to master our appetites. Both of us had been told to go home and lose weight. But both of us had checked out 100 per cent in gall bladder, reflexes, x-rays and tonsils. We felt we could whip the world . . . providing everyone was middle-aged and clumsy.

But we weren't sure we could whip our son's idea of a physical fitness program.

"I will take care of your weight problem," he said with confidence, "but first we will run. I will run with you. We will run two miles and then I will check your heartbeat."

"If I run two miles," I informed him, "I will not have a heartbeat. You will not have to check anything. I will have gone to my reward. My running anywhere will be a waste of time. It also will be a waste of mother."

He pooh-poohed my fears and urged me outside. "But I don't have anything to wear," I complained. "I don't have a cute little red sweatsuit. When they run on TV they don't run in doubleknit slacks and a smock."

He pooh-poohed that, too. But then he was in snappy gray sweats, his tennis shoes flickering in the sunshine. What did he know!

"It's cold. Much too cold to run," I said. "The oxygen in the air is frozen. It won't enter my lungs and I'll suffocate. Let's wait until July."

"It is 70 degrees," he pointed out. "The birds are singing."

Personally, I do not think it should be 70 degrees during the month of March in Nebraska. It never has been. Why did it have to pick this year to be so warm?

My husband was entering into the spirit of things. He was hopping up and down. He thought it was fantastic. He was eager to become virile. I was eager to do anything but run. Anything!

"Golly," I said, "gee, I'm sorry. I'll just have to beg off this time. I have to do your laundry before you go back to school."

"I didn't bring any. Now, let's run!"

So we did. At least I ran a little bit. About four steps. Then I began to huff and to puff like the big bad wolf. My god, I thought, I'll never make it to the corner and I have one mile and 99 hundredths left to go.

My ears were popping. Neighbors were coming out on their front porches, dogs barked and little children jumped in glee. Our three younger girls were taking turns on the telephone calling their friends. They were telling them they could certainly stay out late from now on for their mother would no longer be around to harass them.

Now, I am not against physical fitness. I think it is fine for superstars and sons who major in physical education. As a matter of fact, quite often I do a little exercising myself. I bend down and pet the dog. But I do not run. Not as an every day run-of-the-mill practice.

Under exceptional circumstances, of course, I do run. Very fast. I will run to the basement when a tornado is forcast; I will run to the kitchen if the meat is burning and I will run any-where I can if I see a mouse. But other than that, I limit my pace to a slow shuffle.

So why, I ask myself, am I running down the street for all the neighbors to see? My husband and son were running far ahead of me. Well, my husband was not quite as far ahead as my son. In fact I had begun to notice that his steps were not quite as vital and pounding as they had been when we started. In fact, I noticed they were becoming quite sluggish.

"Come on Pokes!" our son shouted — his cheeks flushed with fresh air and pure good health. My skin tone was becoming alarmingly putty gray and I was yawning a lot. I had heard somewhere that when you yawned a lot it was due to a lack of oxygen. I believed that. I didn't think it was an old wives' tale. I felt my oxygen supply was decidedly low at this point. It was nearly non-existent.

I slowed down my running stomp to a fast walk. Then a medium walk. Then a leaden walk. And then I sat down. "I can go no further," I said out loud. A tiny beetle chuckled. I think we had been racing and he figured he had won!

I looked up the street. My husband was sitting down too. His head in his hands, his feet were making tiny moving motions like Augie-doggie does when he is sleeping and dreaming of running through the fields. His spirit wanted to run, but his body said, "No way!" We were pooped.

Sprinting back, our son stopped in front of his father. They had a heated and lengthy conversation. My husband was baring his teeth. I could see that. They started walking toward me. Occasionally our son would give a little running hop . . . look toward his father . . . his father would shake his head "No" and they continued to approach me at a snail's pace. "By the time they get to me," I promised myself, "I will be breathing again."

"I had a rock in my shoe," I alibied when they stopped in front of me. "I did not want to run the risk of bruising my foot and ending my running forever. I had to sit down and remove the rock." The little beetle giggled. "Just shut up!" I said to him, twanging him with my fingernail. "You won didn't you!"

He scurried off into the bushes wiggling his antennae. Probably had a son in there, somewhere, that was waiting to measure his heartbeat.

"My health view," our son lectured when we had returned to our house and my husband and I were stretched out in our easy chairs and panting, "is that the two of you are definitely out of shape." Until now the two of us had been quite content with the other's shape. We thought they were quite nice. But we could hardly explain this to our son, now could we?

"But running might not be the answer," he continued. Thank God, I breathed.

"How about tennis?" he queried.. "Definitely not," said my husband quickly. "I will not appear in public in short pants for health's sake, your sake or anybody's sake. Tennis is out!"

"Gymnastics?" he asked. "Nope," I vetoed. "I will not stretch my tired old body into gymnastic contortions. That is muscle malpractice at my age. You'll just have to come up with something better if you want to guide us to health and beauty."

His face twisted in careful thought. Somehow his professors had not covered this in their lectures. It had all seemed so simple in the classroom. I felt rather sorry for him. He was only trying to help. And we were proud of him. After all, we had sent him to school to learn and he was doing very well. It wasn't his fault his first experiment in physical fitness centered around two disaster areas.

"Just find something we can handle," I said softly, "and we'll co-operate . . . I promise."

"I'll put you on a diet," he said, brightening considerably. "That's what I'll do. We'll start with a health-filled diet." He looked happy.

My husband and I were happy too. We could cheat on a diet. We always did. We could handle a diet.

"But first I'll need a skin-caliper," he said.

"What's that?" I asked. I thought you just needed a cheap calorie wheel. There's that education again.

"It measures skin folds," he said. "I'll measure your skin folds and then see what your ideal weight is for your particular body frame."

Well, that did it! That ended the physical fitness program for all time.

Nobody is going to measure MY folds. Nobody!

LABOR ON THE LINKS

I am still trying to play golf. Personally, I think it is highly overrated as a sport. A person has to have a touch of manic-depressive in them to walk 90 miles in extreme heat just to hit a little white ball. Or NOT hit the little white ball . . . which is worse.

"It must be my eyesight," I wailed to my husband as I chopped the air for the 40th time and the ball remained stationary on the ground.

"You don't concentrate," he advised. "You have to concentrate. Lean into your swing, keep your eye on the ball, keep your left arm straight, pull your body with your club, relax, follow through, tilt your iron, and don't try to kill the ball."

It is definitely not the ball I am going to kill!

I can't possibly follow all of those directions. It is very difficult. Especially when you can't see. It is very hard to play golf in bifocals. They keep slipping down the bridge of your nose.

"I am too old for this game," I complain as I trudge behind my husband. "I am too old to crawl under cedar trees looking for my ball. I am too old to hop across creeks without falling in. I am too old to go nine holes without a potty stop."

He looks at me and grins. And keeps inviting me to play with him. I still haven't figured out why he does. Or why I accept. You'd think he'd get tired of hearing me grumble. I do.

"Well, I certainly know what I'm going to do," I say to him as I approach my third sand trap of the morning. "I'm going to sell these darn clubs the minute we get back home."

My husband doesn't answer.

"Well," I continue as I putt 11 times on No. 5, "I doubt if anyone would be stupid enough to buy them. I'll just give them to the first person I meet."

He still doesn't answer.

"By God, I'll throw them away," I yell as my drive goes into the rough three feet from the tee.

This time I get his attention.

I realize that I do not have to play golf. No one is forcing me to go out in the hot sun, swing 95 times at the ball and come home sweaty, cross and muscle sore. I can choose to look down at my white ball and say . . . "I give up. You win. I quit!"

But I just can't.

I admit that housekeeping throws me, teenagers often get the best of me, Augie-Doggie is smarter than I am and I can't always make zucchini squash edible. But those are BIG things. Ladies and gentlemen, I am talking about a little white ball against a grown-up woman of 47. Do you really think I'd give in and let it win?

You bet your life I would . . . if my husband would only let me. But he keeps trying to build up my morale.

"Look," he says, as a lady in the next fairway boots her ball and loses it in the weeds. "See, she isn't any better than you and she isn't giving up."

She doesn't have to. She might not be able to play golf any better than I but she sure is straight ahead in other directions. Dressed in tiny, white shorts and red muscle shirt she lifts her tanned arm in pathetic surrender as she hunts for her ball. Fourteen men leap across the course, gunning little electric carts like stock cars to come to her aid. I could crawl around on my hands and knees for three hours and no one would even say goodmorning. I know . . . I've tried it. It is not always how you play the game, I always say, it's how you look when you are playing it.

"Maybe if we had a golf cart to ride around in my game would improve," I whined. "Everyone else is riding — why do we have to walk?"

"For the exercise," my husband answered. "We play golf for the exercise. We are not professionals. We are not earning a living playing the game." (Heaven forbid). "We are here because we NEED the exercise. Riding would ruin the whole purpose of our game.

Better to ruin the purpose than my body, I remind him. He says I exaggerate. I don't think so. But then what do I know. After all a little white ball is smarter than I am.

Just the other day I gave myself one last chance. I approached the ball on the tee and addressed it . . . "OK, little white ball. This is it. This is your final chance!"

I swung my club with all my might. I leaned into it just as I am supposed to. Crack! The little white ball soared through the air. It was perfectly straight.It nestled in the middle of the fairway a respectable distance away. My husband applauded in the background. The lady in the red muscle shirt looked envious. At that point . . . at that particular moment . . . I was smarter than the little white ball!

You know, I think I'll keep my clubs after all.

GARBAGE GHOST RIDES AGAIN

If our family lived next door to the Grand Canyon we'd have it filled with garbage in six weeks. My husband says I am exaggerating. He says we don't have that much stuff. I told him he hadn't been upstairs lately.

I have never been able to understand how some people live in such delicate grandeur without any trace of garbage.

"Where can their garbage be?" I asked my husband on a return trip home from visiting sanitary friends. "I carried this crumpled paper napkin around all night looking for a garbage can."

"Did you look under the kitchen sink?"

"It wasn't there," I answered. "But you should have seen it. You should have seen how neat it was." I wanted to cry. "Did you know she arranges her cleaning supplies alphabetically!"

My husband sighed. This was more than his imagination could handle. It sounded almost like the first step to heavenly home living to him. You see, he is not used to a tidy under-the-sink atmosphere. He is used to reaching his hand into surprises . . . into the enthusiastic mating of oven cleaner and spray paint; rug shampoo and sour dish cloth; furniture polish and scouring pads. He is not used to a quick laying-on-of-hands to anything stashed in the dark and mysterious recesses of our kitchen sink. I am sure he thinks twice about even opening it up. I know I do.

I have always thought it would lend class to our kitchen to put the garbage under the sink like most people do. But our sink would have to be six feel tall in order to accommodate the trash bag comfortably.

"Perhaps you could try emptying it more often," my husband suggested. "Then you could use a smaller sack."

Now that hurt. If there is one thing I do . . . it is empty garbage. I am a compulsive garbage emptier. Or at least, according to the children, I am a compulsive director of garbage emptiers.

Our children seldom say to me, "I have nothing to do" for I say back . . . "Go empty garbage." They are also directed to empty garbage before they leave for a movie, when they return home from a movie, before meals, after meals, before school, after school, before bedtime, after bedtime and during commercials.

However, I do not ask my husband to empty garbage. There is a reason. He brings it all back in.

I have watched him from the window, sorting the garbage . . . examining lettuce leaves for wilt, sniffing through leftovers from the refrigerator, shaking old newspapers to see if I secretly wrapped anything of value, running his fingers over peelings to judge the dimensions of potato left on, holding a cracked glass up to the sun to measure the damage. I have watched him fill his pockets with items "too good to throw away" like a busy squirrel. He would be a mental mess if he lived next door to a garbage dump. He absolutely could not stand to see people throw away so much good stuff.

I think if and when he is reincarnated he will return as a "garbage ghost."

One of my many crosses that I bear in the housekeeping area is the fact we do not have a garbage disposal unit in our kitchen. My husband says it is because he is interested in my personal safety. I am not so sure I fall for that.

"You know how careless you are," he reminded me. "You know how mechanical things confuse you. You know that you would live in 24-hour danger of being swallowed up and spit into the sewer if we had a garbage disposal."

"I'm too big," I said. "You'd find a way," he answered.

I suppose he is right. They are rather terrifying. I've watched them operate. I shudder to think what it would be like to wash your hair in the sink and flip the wrong switch. Why, that thing could eat you up in a minute.

Augie-Doggie would hate it anyway. It would spoil some of the most exciting moments of his day. He adores examining our garbage. He adores lifting the flip-lid and peering in at the contents . . . rummaging through with his paw. He is much like my husband in this respect — except he doesn't have any pockets to put things in.

He adores comparing the dinner I have just cooked and placed in the garbage to his own sacked dog food. He is always hoping to find that our leftovers were better than this food. It usually isn't. He is usually disappointed.

I tell him not to be discouraged. I tell him some day he can join the "garbage ghost" and the two of them can fly through eternity, happily searching for their very own personal heavenly garbage route forever . . . and ever.

He wags his tail . . . like he can hardly wait.

DADDY'S MENU!!

Shueth

PETS ADD TO EASTER JOY!

Easter morning has a way of activating our dog. This dog, who has been content to gnaw bones, eat dried dog food and shake the hands of strangers as they appear on our sidewalk, has a complete turn-about in personality and becomes a snoopy, greedy, artificial grass eating beastie. He runs around most of the morning with bits and pieces of green hanging out of his mouth, with a fuzzy bunny ear or two drooping from the side of his jaw. By noon he has eaten at least four dozen of the carefully hidden eggs and has a chocolate ring around his nostrils. He looks quite sick. In late afternoon he has been joined by the children and more than likely my husband. They, too, have chocolate rings and look sick. Next year I plan to buy evil-tasting eggs. Better still, I'll whip up a batch of my very own, original recipe cookies. That should do it.

Easter lasts a long time at our house. For one thing, I have a permanently embedded vision of various pre-schoolers attending Sunday School in their Easter best (their expensive Easter best) with a marshmallow rabbit crushed to the seats of their pants. No matter what we did, one child always went to church sticky. I don't suppose the Lord minded so much but it sort of took the edge off for mother when she had to spit-clean during the sermon.

Easter continues to continue because we sometimes break down and buy an "Easter Pet." This is usually my idea. My husband has one strong notion about pets. He expects to eat them when they grow up. Naturally he wouldn't eat the dog (who'd want to eat a dog with chocolate nostrils?) or the cat but he had every intention of eating the rabbits and the chickens. Isn't that awful!

We had four rabbits. I bought the rabbits hoping to give the children a lovable, cuddly and cute way of watching Mother Nature at work. My husband bought the rabbits with the purpose of having an inexhaustible supply of meat right at his finger tips. Isn't that awful!

We had a white one, a black one, a brown one and a spotted one. We named them Whitey, Blacky, Browny and Spotty. Naturally.

And because rabbits seem to have the same type of reputation we had, we expected scads of instantaneous baby rabbits. But they were a big bust as far as rabbits go. All they did was sit in their cages, eat carrots and hop. We finally came to the conclusion they were all of one sex or very strange rabbits. It certainly exploded a lot of myths we had heard about rabbits. I finally gave them away one night, when it was dark, while my husband was sharpening his knife in the kitchen. I just sneaked those little rabbits right out from under his mouth. Isn't that awful!

The next Easter we got chickens. We had ten baby chicks and fifty pounds of chicken feed. That's a lot of chicken feed. It's also a lot of chickens, especially when you have no place to put them. We put them in a box in the playpen. The little children thought they were a bunch of new toys. I tried to explain. It was very difficult. The closest the children had ever been to a farm was Mr. Green Jeans. Therefore, when my back was turned, they played with the chicks as if they were mechanical, wind-up toys and not real live, breathing, blood and feather, highly mashable chickens. I will say those little chicks were deeply loved by the children. The little chickens developed the secure feeling of being wanted. Subconsciously I felt pretty bad about this, for I knew their eventual fate.

Very maternally and without premeditated malice, one of the chickens was squeezed around the neck and loved to death. At least it was on the brink. Its eyes rolled back and its head hung. Have you ever heard a chicken gasp? My first aid for chickens was limited but I couldn't just stand there and let it go! I knew right away, however, that mouth-to-mouth was OUT!

I had seen people look like that in old movies on television. Running to the bathroom I grabbed a medicine dropper from the cabinet. Passing through the kitchen, I snatched a bottle of gin. This is what they did on TV and if it was good enough for Gary Cooper it was certainly good enough for a chicken.

I couldn't have given that little chicken more than four or five drops of undiluted gin before it was obvious that the therapeutic value of "gin and chicken" was terrific. It became a virtual dynamo of yellow fluff. It was as happy as a lark. That was one "stoned" little chicken. But it was alive and well. In fact it stayed the healthiest of the ten . . . the first to greet me when I went to scatter feed. I called it "Soak."

My husband said it tasted the best too. Isn't that awful!

WHO NEEDS A DRIVER'S LICENSE, ANYWAY

This has been an exciting time. Our current 15-year-old is learning to drive. To those of you who were born with a silver steering wheel in your mouth, this is no big deal. To the instructor of the Driver's Ed. course, you can bet his life it is! He probably goes home nights and updates his obituary . . . just in case.

Personally, I wouldn't have his job. And frankly, they wouldn't give it to me. My qualifications are a little rancid.

Oh, I have a driver's license. It took me 12 years to get it. I remember when I took driver's training. I was 30 years old and fading. I took it from the calmest, kindest man in the whole world. He was not my husband. He was a specially trained instructor with a specially built training car. It had two brakes and he had nerves of steel.

He let me drive right down town, in the late afternoon traffic, the first evening I was ever behind the wheel of a car. What aplomb he showed as he waved to friends and acquaintances . . . showing me HE was not afraid, and that he had full confidence in my ability as a grown woman with brains. I was pale and beyond recognition. No one waved to me as we ran stop lights. They couldn't tell who the chalk white woman was . . . the chalk white woman whose tension-rusted hands were gripped to the steering wheel permanently and whose right foot was slowly dying of muscle spasms.

It hadn't helped matters when my husband laughed, right out loud, as we pulled away from the curb in front of our house and that the neighbors had brought all of their little children inside the house and watched through the windows. I knew they were there — the cowards.

ANYONE that can read can drive a car, they told me. Well, I could read alright, but I was having real trouble driving that car. I pulled my weight in the ordinary, down-the-street, pause-at-the-stoplight, watch-for-trains sort of driving. It was the insignificant things like backing up, parking and remembering to turn on the signal lights that got to me. And the mere smell of a traffic policemen put me in a panic. I respected the law. Boy, did I respect the law!

The only time my calm, kind driving instructor came unglued was the afternoon I spied a policeman . . . hovering in the dusk . . . three blocks away . . . waiting . . . just waiting. I knew he was waiting for me. I just knew it. I immediately went to pieces. I took my hands from the wheel, covered my eyes, let the muscles spasms in my foot go all the way and stepped on the gas. My instructor screamed! Loud! And in terror!

"MY GOD, HERE COMES A CEMENT TRUCK . . .!" And it truly was. We were both approaching the intersection at the same time. He was sort of lumbering along, as cement trucks are apt to, and I was coming toward him like a bull. Of course, I didn't know this, for I still had my eyes covered. It was my instructor that was so unusually alert. Slamming on the auxiliary brake he brought us to a very, very, very quick stop. I can't remember when I've stopped so fast. The cement truck whizzed on by and as it passed the driver leaned out of the window and screamed something obscene. Imagine . . . yelling at a mother!

But my instructor was a true gentleman. He didn't say anything. He couldn't . . . his swollen tongue was sticking out of his mouth. Softly, and with ashen face he returned me home. For some reason that was my last lesson. He turned me over to my husband. Told him HE could finish up with the unimportant things like backing up, parking and turning on signal lights.

I went through two learner's permits. I didn't have the nerve to get a third. But it really wasn't all my fault. Now tell me, who could learn to drive in an atmosphere of . . . "Watch that car!"; "Turn here now!"; "Keep your eyes on the road!"; "There's a bump here!" "Oh, good grief!" and "Mommy's trying to kill us, isn't she Daddy?"

Oh, eventually I learned to drive. But no one in our family, or my close friends or the dogs will ride with me. I have to rely on perfect strangers if I want company when I'm driving. Sometimes I get very lonesome.

A HAIRY HOROSCOPE

For years I have believed that my day's destiny was controlled by little things . . . little homely things. If, for instance, I am able to down the first cup of coffee of the day before the kitchen raid starts . . . surely things are going to go fine. If everyone finds clean and matching socks at one crack . . . the day has to be good. If I have enough small change to go around for various athletic events, assembly programs and seconds in the lunchline without writing ten checks for 15 cents each . . . it's all going along fine.

On the other hand, when I hop out of bed and discover the dog has been left in all night and shouldn't have been . . . things don't look so good. If I forget to put the lid on the blender when I push the mix button for orange juice . . . I'd rather scratch the whole day. And when I take a quick peek in the mirror after eating all that tuna fish and I STILL can't see where my ribs end and my hips begin . . . it's bound to be rotten all around.

That's the way I used to pace my day. Evidently, I've been going at it all wrong. According to some people I should read my horoscope and let it manipulate my day. There is just one problem. I can't always understand my horoscope well enough to know what I'm supposed to do with myself. Sometimes a whole day passes and I'm still not sure what I should have done.

I certainly don't have time to just sit around and try to decipher things like "your sign coincides with the festival of Muharras, in which men in tiger costumes stage processions to celebrate the strength and fortitude of the grandsons of the gods." I really can't see where men running around in tiger suits has anything to do with MY day. I suppose it would be interesting to see and all that, but it doesn't help me decide whether to wash the walls in the dining room or blow the whole afternoon playing bridge.

I just wish it would be more specific. Why can't it just say I might cut my jugular vein on the can opener or drop the iron on my big toe or meet a mouse going down the basement steps instead of skirting around with "until the 20th guide against mishaps." Well, I want you to know, I spend a miserable 20 days. I am afraid of my shadow. Make my family nervous wrecks. Everytime someone opens the door or the telephone rings or they drop a notebook . . . I scream.

Once in awhile, though, I will have to admit that old horoscope comes pretty close. I'd hardly put down the one that read "a clutching and lively period in which you overcome handicaps and reach compromises that pave the way for greater serenity" to dress for a noon luncheon when I discovered the only pair of pantyhose left in the house was three sizes too small for me. It was a clutching and lively period while I was attempting to put them on. The compromise came when they split up the middle and I decided to wear them anyway. Actually, I was quite serene in the knowledge that no one could see the split anyway!

I have learned to interpret some of them though . . . Ones like "don't in your enthusiasm make statements you can't substantiate or promises you may not be able to keep!" means "Don't volunteer your husband to chaperone a junior high dance."

"A sticky home situation will not be solved easily" scares some people into thinking of serious and terrible family problems. I just know that one of the children has been eating bread and honey in the living room and knocked the honey jar over on the carpet.

If mine says "Great fame will come to you" it probably indicates that I will be pregnant when I'm 58 years old. Or when it says "people will be traveling to you, from a distance for financial or reunion reasons," I don't get all excited and run about changing sheets or opening new savings accounts at the bank — our college son is just coming home for the weekend to ask for money and for a reunion with the washing machine.

The one I really don't like is "Save your money, it is just not your time for spending." My husband had them put that in there . . . I just know he did.

Once in awhile I should pay attention. Once in awhile I shouldn't think I'm smarter than my horoscope. Next time it says "be wary of travel . . . stay home!" I'm going to do it. I'm not going to go over the county line with the gas tank on empty and have the car stall, overheat and have a flat tire . . . all at one time and just have to sit there for an hour and cry because no one came along to help me and it was before the 20th and I was afraid to get out and walk.

I sure could have used those fellows in the tiger suits THAT day.

IT ISN'T ALWAYS WISE TO LIE!

Once upon a time, a few years ago, when we were going through our "isn't it nice to live in the country and smell all this fresh air" stage, we inherited, by accident on our part and intention on some smart person's, a little fat, gray puppy. My husband claimed he knew, all along, things weren't as they should be . . . that little, fat puppy was, underneath it all, a full-grown dog. He suggested we do something constructive . . . immediately . . . like get rid of her.

"Oh, no!" I cried. "Little puppies do not eat much and look how she wags her tail when I pat her head." My husband was not impressed.

Little puppy and I became conspirators. I taught her to hide in the shed when my husband was home and to frisk about only when his car left the driveway. He thought little puppy was gone. I knew better. So did little puppy.

Little puppy thrived. She grew and grew and bulged and bulged. Even I became suspicious that she might have a problem. Eventually she had four problems.

"Now what?" my husband asked the morning he discovered that little puppy had not left the premises for another home like we had led him to believe — and that the whimpering in the shed meant more puppies not less.

I had no answer for him. At least, not at that moment. But an answer was to come. Heaven has a way of protecting little puppies and wives that lie! Sometimes.

Big Brown Rooster solved all of my problems. Big Brown Rooster was my husband's mistake. I hate chickens. I do not even like their eggs. I did not want Big Brown Rooster. Even if he was a thoroughbred, full-blooded, brown-spotted Wyandotte or whatever.

"But look at his majesty," my husband pointed out when the people offered to give us Brown Rooster. "Look how he struts."

I hoped he would strut right out of the yard. He didn't. He hung around. He hung around the hens and he hung around the clothesline, he hung around the garbage can and he hung around the back porch. And he hung around people. He especially hung around people. He liked to attack them.

The three little girls were terrified. They wouldn't even go to the chicken house to collect eggs anymore. They barely ventured outside for the mail. I wouldn't hang sheets or empty garbage. I compared little gray puppy to that Rooster.

"At least little gray puppy isn't a potential murderer," I said. "Brown Rooster has blood in his eyes."

"He's just fiesty," my husband said proudly. He sounded envious. "Don't worry about Brown Rooster. He'll get along."

But one day . . . one day . . . Brown Rooster made a mistake. He bit my husband. Right in the back of the leg — when his back was turned.

Immediately things began to happen.

My husband stalked in the house. The blood was now in his eyes. Brown Rooster had gone too far. This time he had bitten the wrong fellow. My husband grabbed his gun. I don't know what kind of gun he grabbed. It was long and had bullets. He put the bullets in his pocket.

"What are you going to do?" I asked sweetly and with just enough innocence. Little gray puppy was smiling and thumping her tail.

"I'm going to shoot that chicken!" he shouted. Brown Rooster wasn't even a Rooster anymore . . . he was just a chicken.

I didn't ask how many bullets it took. I didn't say a word. I just know that for weeks the hens didn't lay any eggs and would hardly come out of the henhouse for water. It must have been some battle.

Little gray puppy lived at our house for many months. So did her four puppies. The puppies were very cute and not housebroken.

It didn't take long for me to decide that maybe I wasn't so smart after all!

PRINCESS FOR AN EVENING

I was born to be a princess . . . I just know I was. Why, then, do I look and feel like a frog?

It's my environment. I know it is. Of course, I would function more regally if I was surrounded by an atmosphere of velvet and gold instead of chenille and clear plastic.

Can you imagine a princess washing her comely face before a mirror streaked with toothpaste? Or being buried hip-high in an automatic dryer 40 per cent of her life? Or discovering the dog has been groomed with her hairbrush? Or reaching her highest level of excitement when she finds all the socks match? Or choosing her wardrobe from a mail-order catalog?

And speaking of wardrobes . . . have you ever seen a tubby princess? Well, I haven't. I firmly believe royal bones automatically melt fat. Obviously, my more common bones gobble up flesh and stack it in layers.

It must be a state of mind that keeps a princess so skinny. I suppose if I had to glide everywhere I went and wear a tiara I'd stay skinny too. But no one expects anything like that from me. I don't even own a tiara. If I thought it would help, I'd certainly make out an order for one.

I practiced being a princess just the other night. I wanted to see how it felt. I didn't expect anything permanent . . . but I thought it might be fun for a while.

We had finished a kingly dinner of pizza and chocolate chip ice cream and I was on the couch sewing a strap on a pair of overalls when I felt an exquisite light encircle my head.

"You are a princess," a tiny voice said.

I almost felt the tip of a wand touch my shoulder.

With a shake of my head, a flip of my foot and the tingling toss of my fingers (trying very hard to grow fingernails in a split second) I shifted into "glamorous" and began my princessly slide across the floor.

"Why are you walking like that?" my husband asked, glancing up from the evening paper. "Does your back hurt again? Take an aspirin."

"Prithee, good sire, what is your pleasure?" I asked in a dainty and cultivated voice.

"Huh?"

With a tinkling laugh and a toss of my long, flowing mane (well, as much as you can toss a blow-cut), I raked my fingers along his cheek.

"Ouch!"

"I will refresh you, good sire," I said, turning delicately on my toe and nearly pitching headlong into the television.

I willowed my way through the room, trying desperately to keep my hips from spreading.

I fixed iced tea and potato chips — not too neat a fare to offer a prince, but that's all I could find.

I sat down beside him, making a circle with my glass, sniffing the contents. I'd seen people do this when they were tasting vintage wines.

"What's wrong with the iced tea?" he asked suspiciously as he glanced into his glass.

"Nothing, good sire," I answered, trying hard to keep a princess-like quality to my tone of voice. This wasn't turning out at all like I had expected.

"You certainly are acting strange," he said. "Is it that over-40 business again?"

"It bothers me that I'm not a princess," I whimpered. "I thought it would be nice for you if I were a princess."

"So that's it," he said. "Can't you get it through your head that if I had wanted a princess for a wife I would have married one?"

I didn't know he knew any! He sure had me fooled.

I crunched a potato chip and was content. The pressure was off. I didn't have to be a princess anymore. In a way, I was sorry. I was beginning to enjoy myself . . .

Later that evening as we were settling down for the night, my husband questioned my tossing and turning in bed.

"Now what's wrong?" he yawned. "Can't you get to sleep?"

"There's just one thing that's bothering me," I answered, plumping my pillow for the 89th time.

"What's that?"

"Who put the pea under our mattress?"

You see, I don't give up easily.

CLEANING FRIDGE IS FAMILY AFFAIR

Cleaning the refrigerator is not one of my favorite pastimes. I'd almost rather play golf. Almost. And I have to admit that I put it off. But I don't think it is quite as bad as my husband claims it is. I don't think he has to go so far as to threaten to list the contents of our refrigerator in my obituary along with my survivors. I don't think he has to go that far, do you?

Quite often when I get up in the morning and have to spend 30 minutes looking for the milk carton amid the debris I vow to get the whole mess cleaned up before dinner. But, unfortunately, my day is so full of important things I have trouble working cleaning the refrigerator into my schedule. After all, someone at our house has to sort the straight pins, rearrange the kleenex in its box, watch for the mailman, observe the plants growing and drop used razor blades down into the slot in the medicine cabinet. After all, if I didn't do these things, who would! I just don't have time for things like refrigerators. You can see that.

But the other day circumstances were such that I thought maybe I should give it some serious consideration. I missed the cat! And there was a smell in the refrigerator. It couldn't be the cat, I told myself, the cold air circulating would prevent something like that. I was almost sure. But I didn't want to take any chances. I didn't want my husband rummaging around in there looking for lettuce and coming up with a Siamese. I knew he would over-react to something like that and my obituary just might appear before I was ready for it to be written.

Pulling on rubber gloves and donning a plastic apron, I approached the refrigerator. When I work I work in style. I just don't go at it willy-nilly . . . and besides, I was afraid there might be something in there that was so strong and so potent it would dissolve my skin. I wanted to be protected.

"Mom's going to clean the refrigerator," our youngest daughter called up the stairs to her brothers and sisters. "Come and watch! It'll be fun!"

"Maybe my car keys are in there," our son said, bolting down the stairs two at a time. "I lost them three weeks ago. I've looked everywhere."

"Is she going to swear?" the other son said. "I need some new words to keep up with my class."

He was in junior high. TV had been failing him lately. I suppose he needed inspiration and thought I might provide it.

The children gathered in the kitchen. The dog ran to join them. The cat strolled in.

"Boy, am I glad to see you," I said, stooping to pet her back. She purred and stood, licking her lips, at the refrigerator door. I was doing her thing.

I filled a bucket with sudsy, antiseptic water, flipped my clean rag in the air, smoothed down my plastic apron and flexed my gloved fingers. I was ready. Like a perfectly honed surgeon I began the removal of the sordid contents with skillful artistry.

Out of the refrigerator came six catsup bottles ... all partially empty and all with an accumulation of catsup on the neck of the bottle and squishing under the cap and down the sides; one plastic egg of silly putty; one sticky honey jar with honey frozen stiff; one can of chocolate syrup accompanied by chocolate running down the can, down the refrigerator door, down on the carrots and down on the carpet; two bowls of popcorn; one strong, ripe onion; three broken eggs; an empty pop bottle; eight empty bowls; a box of graham crackers; four toast-crumbed sticks of oleo; a turnip that had sprouted; a green sock; a can of frozen beer; a can of melted orange juice; a piece of Christmas candy; some gray tuna fish; four balloons; a portion of pale, poisonous potato salad; some terrible looking stuff that I couldn't recognize or remember and a set of car keys.

"Hurrah!" our son said, grabbing the car keys and running out the door to his car. "I'll be back for dinner," he called over his shoulder.

"Good!" I yelled, "we're having leftovers."

"I'll eat out," he answered. "So will I," said our other son. "So will I," said each of the other children. "So will I," said the cat.

"HA HA," I said. I closed the door on the shiny and sparkling refrigerator and went to the store. I bought two succulent T-bones, some mushrooms, some gourmet salad dressing and iceberg lettuce, a bottle of wine and two white candles. My husband and I had a wonderful dinner ... quiet, nice, just the two of us.

Cleaning the refrigerator has some fringe benefits after all.

69

TEN RULES FOR MOVING

I certainly do like to move. The thrill of seeing the people next door react as two pretty crummy looking adults, seven pretty crummy looking children and one very crummy looking dog (we sneak the cats in after dark) spew forth from the front of a U-Haul truck never wears off. I don't tell them we are nice people and that I do have dress-up clothes. I let them guess. I also let them guess how many of us there really are. This provides parlor games in the neighborhood for days.

I feel keeping my composure on moving day is just as important as putting a blanket over the furniture as we move it from the truck to the house. I certainly don't want anyone to see our furniture in stark sunlight nor do I want anyone to see me lose my temper and have strangers witness one of my mother-of-a-large-family fits. They can be outstanding. I truly did want to do everything right but it isn't easy when on moving day everyone turned into miniature evil spirits at the breakfast table.

Our oldest daughter, for instance, insisted she could not eat one more bite if she had to look at her brother. She went on to explain that she had learned in school that mother guppies ate their young. She further explained that I had made a serious mistake when I failed to gobble "him" up immediately after birth. Her brother aimed a ferocious kick to the shins in her direction. It veered off to the left, catching his father right below the knee. This caused more commotion than any of us planned on.

During this commotion a cereal box was upset and removed from the table. This caused another daughter to become upset and to, also, be removed from the table. As she left she sobbed . . . "I was reading that box. I had just about decided what to buy you for Mother's Day." I sneaked a peek. She had two choices. The premiums offered for $1.98 and three boxtops included a set of Disneyland posters and an avocado green, plastic tablecloth with fringe. My conscience told me I should be ashamed . . . the aesthetic in me applauded.

Tears were streaming down the face of our youngest son. He had realized . . . finally . . . that he was soon to be parted from his true-blue buddy Terry, an inseparable duo since blanket days. One child cried because she wanted chocolate stars for breakfast instead of orange juice and one cried in her high

70

chair because everyone else was crying. The child left over, the child who was not complaining, crying or kicking . . . the one who was quietly stealing and eating everyone else's bacon eventually caused more complaining, crying and kicking than anyone else. I was tired of moving and hadn't even started wrapping the breakables in newspapers.

This is when I drew up my list of rules. This is when I insisted they be on their best behavior. This is when I explained that first impressions are lasting and if we made ourselves inconspicuous and well-mannered there might be an outside chance people would not panic and start putting out "For Sale" signs. I lined them up against the wall and reviewed these rules.

RULES FOR MOVING DAY

1 — Do not greet the Welcome Wagon lady with "What did you bring us?"

2 — Do not run around outside or answer the door naked. This applied mostly to those under five. After kindergarten they became so modest they hid behind the door to blow their nose.

3 — Do not invite anyone over six into the house without first coming to check with me. I do not want to be caught down on my hands and knees . . . swearing . . . as I unpack broken breakables by new people.

4 — Do not accept a bribe of cookies in order to sneak anyone into the house to observe me without checking first.

5 — Do not gallop out the door screaming "She's going to kill me . . . please, help! She's going to kill me!" I know and you know that you are talking about your two older sisters but people will get the wrong idea. They will get the idea you mean your gentle mother.

6 — Do not spill garbage in the driveway.

7 — Do not go up and down the street ripping off mailboxes. This, too, applied mostly to under five year olds. They liked playing mailman.

8 — Do not immediately set up a kool-aid stand and tell people you are helping buy groceries.

9 — Do not take Augie-Doggie around to introduce him. They'll all learn who he is soon enough.

10 — Do not leave the yard for any reason except school for the next three weeks. This is an important rule and must be obeyed. People automatically think "stampede" when they count over three children and start to build chain-link fences.

I insisted my husband listen to these rules too. I didn't really worry that he would suddenly burst forth naked or ask the Welcome Wagon lady for presents and I told him he could leave the yard without permission but I didn't tell him he could leave for one whole week . . . and that's just what he did. He took a business trip.

I noticed that he packed happily and smiled a lot when he boarded the plane. Missed all the fun at home, too.

HOODOO OF HOME REPAIR

I sincerely admire those members of the sisterhood who can stalk into a hardware store, ask for a Phillips screwdriver and know when the salesman hands them one it isn't Donald's or Ralphs's or George's but good old Phillip's.

My husband says I take home repair jobs too seriously. I get too up-tight about them. He is well aware that I have reached my level of incompetency when the pilot light goes out in the oven.

Usually when he is home this is no real problem. I just voluptuously slither up to him, match in hand, and toss out a low-vibrating, "Dear, will you help?" He immediately jumps into action — not because of the voluptuous slithering or vibrating voice but he knows I have a roast in the oven and he does not want to eat it raw and bleeding.

When he is not here I often have quite a bit of trouble. You see, I have always been under the impression (due to early childhood teachings) that anyone who monkeys around with matches is going to have problems at bedtime. Therefore, it is against all my principles to play with fire. Even if it is self-contained at the bottom of the stove. One hiss from the gas valve and I explode!

I envy the carefree, brave housewive who can march right up to her stove, turn the knob, strike a match, lean back and get instant, controlled temperatures. Often I feel I can do the same thing. I even practice being brave in front of the mirror. Then I remember how frightened I am of explosions.

My husband says my approach is all wrong. He says I am too timid. He says I should stride right up to that oven and show it who's boss. I know who is boss. So does the oven. I don't fool that oven for one minute. It knows I am a coward the second I try to find the right spot to light with my eyes squeezed shut.

But it is a different matter with the hammer. I am not afraid of the hammer. After all, what can a hammer do?

This does not mean, though, that I whisk about engaging in carpentry projects. I have this fear of heights. Climbing more than three inches off the floor makes me dizzy. But I did want to try and prove a point to my family — prove that as a grown-up, independent woman with brains, I could become self-

72

sufficient and put up a silly curtain rod in the kitchen without begging for help.

Armed with hammer, nails, curtain rod, determination and Phillip's screwdriver, I mounted the kitchen stool placed strategically near the window.

But I did not know what to do with the nails. My husband sticks them in his mouth. I tried that and punctured my cheek. I found another place to stash them — fast.

"Measure, measure, measure," I have heard my husband shout when instructing our sons. So I measured. I measured three times and came out with a different answer each time. Finally, I just started to pound.

The pounding vibrated throughout the neighborhood. A crowd gathered below my stool. Everyone wanted to watch. The dog even left his romantic pursuits toward the poodle next door. I thought that was carrying things too far. I wasn't going to be that interesting. At least I didn't want it to be.

"Why are you using five nails when one will do?" my husband asked.

"So it will stay," I answered, taking the sixth nail from my hair where I had parked it. "If a job is worth doing it is worth doing right."

"Well, it will certainly stay," he replied, his mustache quivering with unconcealed mirth. "In fact that curtain rod will be there forever and ever and ever. Just like it is now. Crooked."

He was right. It was crooked. But it was up, wasn't it? And if you leaned your head to the left, parallel to your shoulder, it didn't look half-bad.

So, as far as I'm concerned, if anyone wants to go into my kitchen and gape at my curtain rod they can just tilt their head like I do.

Personally, I think it looks grand.

OF HUSBANDS AND HOSPITALS

Recently my husband spent a few days in the hospital. I realize this particular bit of news is not outstanding. I realize this type of thing happens all the time. But not to my husband.

As for me . . . due to seven babies, a bad back and one or two little lady operations, a trip to the hospital has been as common as germs. The people at the admissions desk don't even take my name — they just wave me on through. My husband had never been a patient before . . . always a visitor.

I think God knew what He was doing.

I have to admit my husband has been a superb visitor. His bedside manner is marvelous. He sends flowers, visits twice a day and brings me a sack of jellybeans. He assures me that things are going well at home — even if they aren't, lets me choose the TV programs, listens sympathetically to my complaints, envys me just a little because I am resting and he is not and eats my jellybeans.

Now it was my turn to prove that I can be a good visitor too. Now HE is the patient. I get to bring new pajamas, robe and slippers, the supply of fresh magazines, the crossword puzzle books and the bag of jellybeans.

Walking into his darkened hospital room I gently kissed him on the cheek. He was sleeping.

"How are you feeling?" I really wanted to know.

"I want to go home!"

A nurse came into the room. She was about my age . . . friendly, sweet. She shook down the thermometer and asked, "How are you feeling?"

"I want to go home!"

"Look," I said, trying to cheer him up. "See the cute cards you have. People are thinking of you. Isn't that nice?"

"I want to go home!"

"Do you want a jellybean?"

"I want to go home!"

"Smell the flowers?"

"I want to go home!"

"The dog threw up in the living room . . . in your big chair!"

"I want to go home!"

"The kids had 23 of their friends over for popcorn. It was terrible. They played all the records you hate on the stereo. They played them very loud. The neighbors complained and the police dropped by."

"I want to go home!"

"Your garden is weedy!"

"I want to go home!"

"It's awful hot outside. Windy and dusty and dry. You can hardly go outside without choking. You are very lucky to be in here where it is cool, calm, clean and moist."

"I want to go home!"

"We aren't eating too much. Last night we had radishes and peanut butter sandwiches. You are very lucky to be in here where you get three good meals a day . . . served to you on a tray. My goodness, you know I don't do that for you at home. ha, ha."

Slight hesitation. "I want to go home!"

"My sister was here from Illinois. She brought her five boys. They were here four days."

Another slight hesitation. "I want to go home!"

"The people next door gave the kids a goat."

"I want to go home!"

"All we get in the mail are bills."

"I want to go home!"

"The kids need new shoes. I have to take them shopping for new shoes. Two of them say they want chukka boots. I don't think I'll be able to talk them out of it. We'll have another big fight in the store. I will miss you!"

"I want to go home!"

The doctor walks in. He is accompanied by a young, fresh-looking nurse. She has soft blonde hair, large pearl-like teeth. She is smiling. She is smiling too much. She is smiling at my husband. Her bosom is high, firm and taut. She is resting a clipboard on her bosom. I do not understand how she can write down the doctor's orders with the clipboard so far away. My husband looks as if he is running a high fever. Suddenly!

"Well, well, well," the doctor says. "And how are we feeling today?"

"I have this pain, Doc" my husband says, "right here. It hurts bad. I don't think I'll ever get well."

"Personally, I think he should go home," I said.

CHILDREN LOVE TO HAVE
DADDY BABYSIT

I certainly did not marry my husband because he came recommended to me as a dependable and reliable babysitter. This, of course, would have been a plus in his favor but at the time I did not even think about it. I wish I had. At the time I concentrated on his broad shoulders, the fact that he smelled good, had a deep voice and looked terrific in a leather jacket. I didn't even think about what kind of babysitter he would make. I bet you didn't think about that either. Boy, did we make a mistake!

Most children love to have daddy babysit. It means total liberty to eat tomorrow's cookies, watch violence on TV, go to bed in their sweatshirts and underwear — at midnight — without a bath — and to paint the neighbor's house with black paint.

My husband has always claimed I over-react to my job of caring for children.

"It should be a joyful task," he said, "one that all parties take pleasure and rejoice in."

I do not understand. He has a mechanism that allows him to turn off any disagreements between our children. To him, their bickering is just the merry pitter-patter of little voices. He is able to read the paper in deep concentration as they choose their weapons and set about to destroy our home ... and each other.

While he reads the sports page they plot each other's immediate death. By the time he has gone through the financial page, taken a short nap and had two bottles of cold beer, one child has locked herself in the bathroom, cowers behind the shower curtain and falls asleep in the bathtub. Another has fled to the safety of the nearest neighbor and is filling them in on the family scandals. One is calling his teacher and telling her he won't be in school for awhile because of the awful bruises he has received at home, and two have run off to Texas. Their father will not know they have gone until mealtime.

It has been a most delightful afternoon for all concerned.

Every mother pays the price of an evening out ... in one way or the other. She has to weigh what she wants more: a night off or three days of concentrated housecleaning when she returns. Most mothers will choose the night off hoping that a miracle will occur and her guardian angel will fly down and babysit in her husband's place. Usually she doesn't. No guardian angel wants to get mixed up in a mess like that ... not if she's worth her heavenly salt.

I used to prepare for a night out as carefully as a general prepares for battle. It took eight hours of careful concentration so I could be gone for three. I would leave a note for my husband when I left ...

"The baby's bottle is prepared and labeled as to quantity and time it should be served. It is in the refrigerator and I have painted it bright green so you cannot make any mistakes. Please do not allow the toddler to eat the dog's food. I realize putting her down to the dog's dish and letting her eat beats trying to push creamed spinach down her throat, but dog food has few people vitamins and my record for no rickets in our children has been good. I would like to keep it that way.

I have never allowed and will never allow, no matter what they say, the two boys to sleep in the nude. I do not think it is very upper class. Tell them they have to wear flannel pajamas just like everyone else. (I realize there are a few exceptions to that rule but I'd not go into it ... I do not believe we owe the children an explanation about THAT!).

Oh, by the way, the child who grasps his throat and chokingly cries out for "water-water," after going to bed, is not dying from thirst but is the one I have cut off from liquids after 8 p.m. for "you-know-what-reason." And last of all, please, PLEASE do not let them eat the fortune cookies I have hidden behind the furnace. They are for my club's foreign tasting tea and it took me days to get them together. Do have a fun night and I will see you later."

When I came home that evening I found the green bottle still in the refrigerator, full and swelling with formula. The baby was sleeping soundly, a smile on her face and a vanilla wafer clutched in her hand. The dog's dish was empty and Augie-Doggie was standing wistfully in front of the icebox . . . begging for something to eat.

"Sorry, fellow," I said. "There's nothing left in here but creamed spinach. Want some?"

The boy's flannel pajamas were strewn across the bedroom floor. Bony, bare bottoms peeked from beneath their covers and the parched kid evidentally had quenched his thirst to his utmost satisfaction, his teddy bear was floating down the hallway.

"The final blow," I said to myself, "will be finding my fortune cookies gone."

I rushed to the basement. Fluttering from the pipes overhead, near the furnace, were dozens of slips of paper. I reached up and grabbed on. It read . . .

"Sorry, I took the day off.
    Your Guardian Angel."

Next time I ask their dad to babysit I'm going to ask for references.

"GIRL GUESTS ARE THE BEST"

Last week our son called from college . . . "Hi, Mom."

"Hi, son." Our dialogue is smashingly brilliant.

"Can I bring a friend home for the weekend?" he said.

"Fine," I answered — mentally counting the pork chops, the steaks and the hamburger in the freezer. I wanted to be sure I had plenty for their breakfast the first day. I know how much boys eat. I could always dash off to the store and buy more stuff before lunch.

I remembered the spot on the living room carpet. Oh well, that didn't matter at all. Boys aren't interested in spots . . . they are only interested in pork chops, steak and hamburger. And a sleeping bag and warm blanket will be fine. Boys don't care where they sleep . . . they only care about pork chops, steaks and hamburger.

"Sure, bring him home," I repeated with a smile.

"He's a GIRL!" our son said smugly.

"Oh, a GIRL!" I sweated. I didn't faint or become hysterical or throw the phone out the window. Give me credit. "Oh, a GIRL!" I didn't know he knew any girls. I thought he was in college to study. That's what he says he does all the time. How did he manage to get to know a girl well enough to ask her home for the weekend? He sure fooled me.

Quickly I took inventory again. I wondered what does a girl eat for breakfast — a strange girl who has never been in our home before . . . a girl who obviously has impeccable and marvelous personal taste (after all, she picked our son out of thousands) — a girl who has never eaten my cooking before.

I know what my own girls eat for breakfast: cereal and vanilla wafers; and I know what I used to eat when I was in college — soda pop and graham crackers . . . but jeez, I couldn't feed her anything like that.

An omelet? That's nice, except I don't know how to make an omelet.

Tiny sausages and perfect eggs? Exceptional, but the cat jumps up on the table whenever he smells sausages frying. That wouldn't do. I suppose I could always serve tea and cinnamon toast, I decided. That's certainly dainty enough.

"She's a University swimmer," he explained. Lord, she'll probably spend a lot of time in the bathtub, I thought. (Buy Bab-bo, I remind myself).

"She's from a small family," he continued. (Farm out four or five children, picked at random, to friends and neighbors).

"She's very nice," he concluded. (Order wedding cake, small mints and check on boutonnieres for ushers). My husband told me I was getting ahead of myself.

It was obvious I had an awful lot to do before the weekend, and 48 hours looked mighty slim. I wondered how I could paint the inside and outside of the house, build a fireplace in the living room, add a bathroom, carpet the entire upstairs, wallpaper one or two rooms, replace all of our furniture, learn to set an elegant table, teach those children I decided to keep home some instant manners, become a gracious mother to our son, become a gracious hostess to the girl, conquer my fear of water so I could discuss swimming without shuddering and becoming nauseous, spay the cat so there wouldn't be any funny stuff, persuade my husband to wear a tie all weekend instead of hopping into his earthy jumpsuit in addition to painting the dandelions green so they would blend with the grass. I was really going to be busy before the weekend. I could see that.

Of course, I didn't get any of it done. Somewhere (after I washed and starched a pair of curtains) I got hard-boiled. And calloused. And tired.

"She'll just have to take us as we are," I announced to my

husband. "All of us." Our present son-in-law knew all along what he was getting into when he married our daughter. He certainly can't throw that up to anybody. "It's better she finds out now than later," I added.

"It's just a weekend visit not holy matrimony," my husband said, as he threw his tie in the closet and dressed in his crummy jumpsuit.

They came on Friday evening. My husband I had a date to play bridge.

"Would you like for us to stay home and keep you company?" I smiled in my very best 'mother-is-going-to-keep-a-good-eye-on-you' smile. "We can play monopoly."

I did not think it was necessary for them to roll on the floor in laughter, hold their sides like idiots, point their fingers and shake their heads. I thought they taught college students to respect their elders. With all that tuition and all. Besides, it wasn't that funny.

"Let's go play bridge," my husband said.

"Call me if you need me," I whispered, slipping the phone number to the little girls. I raised my eyebrows for emphasis. I didn't know if they understood or not. I just had to hope.

We came home early. They were all playing monopoly on the dining room table . . . and eating popcorn.

"See," my husband said. I saw.

It was a very successful weekend. She accepted us and we loved her.

I couldn't have done better if I had picked her out myself.

"ON MY HONOR"

I certainly do remember when our first daughter was a Brownie Scout. Boy, did she shine. She had a bright and beautiful brown uniform. It fit her perfectly. It was hemmed nicely and everything. Her orange tie was starched and knotted symmetrically, her little Brownie beanie sat on her head in military perfection, her brown cuffed socks rose straight above her matching oxfords, her Brownie pin was kept neatly in the jewelry box, polished once a week and it was never, never lost. And she never failed to wear her Brownie smile.

By the time we reached the fifth daughter, the hand-me-down uniform had lost its wash and wear qualities. It sat in the dryer and curdled into a million wrinkles. Each time it was washed there was a definite danger that it would disintegrate and disappear into the lint filter.

And it certainly didn't fit well. This daughter was three inches taller and a few pounds heavier than the others. The uniform barely covered her panties with the hem completely out. And the collar when buttoned caused her to gag. It didn't really matter about the collar anyway for we couldn't find the tie — hadn't seen it for years.

Her beanie was creased and had lost its pointer. There was one brown sock and she usually wore tennis shoes. The Brownie pin had gone through the dryer so many times it had practically melted but she kept her Brownie smile . . . that is what is so nice about Brownie Scouts . . . they smile a lot.

Girls in scouting usually do not begin to grumble and moan until they are in third year Junior Girl Scouts. They are ready for the next level, Cadettes, and their leader is ready for an institution.

It is a false rumor that children benefit from having mothers that serve as Scout leaders. Just ask mine. They thought it was going to be great at first. They visualized being singled out from all the rest and being the Big Wheel that got to carry the flag.

How mistaken they were and how stricken they were when they found out the kindly little lady that gently tucked them into bed at night turned into an ugly, malignant rule shouter the minute that she donned a uniform. After one or two meetings they were begging to be transferred into another troop. More often than not I was ready to sign the transfer papers.

But we had a problem. They could not find a troop to transfer to. Not in the neighborhood anyway. There was a reason for this. No one wanted to be the leader.

It is practically a proven fact that nearly all children who join scouting organizations are orphans the minute their parents sign the permission slip. If you want to see a busy parent . . . talk to a parent with a scout. She has as many excuses as there are germs in a Cub Scout Den.

"I'm sorry," she'd say when I called, "I can't take the girls to the museum. I really must iron." I wonder what she thought that mountain was in my utility room . . . the Adirondacks?

"I'm pregnant," she'd sometimes sigh. So was I usually.

"I don't know a thing about Scouts!" Good heavens, neither did I.

"Children make me nervous." Who don't they make nervous?

"I have new furniture." Well, she had me there . . . I hardly had new anything . . . at least not all at the same time.

"I'm just not interested." And I wasn't interested in her either. And you could bet your Brownie promise she was the first one to complain if the meeting didn't last for three hours and if I didn't bring her child home in the car when the temperature dropped below 75 degrees.

Don't get me wrong. All mothers were not this way. Many, many of them left their dishes in the sink and fed their husbands cornflakes for dinner, pitched right in and danced around as many Brownie rings and stood in as many Girl Scout friendship circles as I did. Some of my best friends have been Girl Scout mothers.

Personally, I have never been able to understand why the ordinary, average person thinks that having a Girl Scout meeting is dull. The kids know better than that and this could be one of the reasons why they join in the first place. They certainly know what fun it is to watch an adult unravel right before their eyes. Where else could they find such cheap entertainment?

I did not have the benefit of workshops or training sessions or this type of thing when I became a leader. I was given a pamphlet, a handbook and the kiss of death by the scout office. Once in awhile they threw in a song book.

I understand this has all changed. Now they have training sessions for prospective leaders. I'm sure it is much more beneficial but I bet some of the excitement is gone.

There were 18 girls in my first troop of Girl Scouts. I still look back on these days and think they were the finest group of girls that ever donned those little berets. They were 11 and 12 years old and more interested in Boy Scouts than Girl Scouts. They are 25 and 26 now and probably still have that problem.

At our first meeting we played little get-acquainted games and I was very polite. So were they. After the first meeting we began to get more serious. I got cross and they giggled and whispered a lot.

One thing I learned early as a leader was to talk very fast. It was not actually necessary to say anything but as long as I was talking they couldn't. That was a rule.

It is a well-known fact that a girl of 12 if given the chance will talk for an unlimited amount of time. My husband does not think that this well-known fact is absolutely confined to 12 year old girls . . . he thinks I do a lot of it now. But then, what does he know?

Nor, I found out, does a leader ever want to ask a direct question. Each girl has a different answer . . . a long, involved different answer. This can eat up the alloted time of the meeting and the girls will go home and complain that all they did at the scout meeting was sit around and talk. And then their mothers will complain and will be disappointed. They expected their daughter to make at least one beaded dress with matching mocassins at the first two meetings. My goodness, what was that lazy, volunteer leader thinking of?

I was very, very nervous when I was a brand-new scout leader. I did not want to make any mistakes and leave the impression with the Girl Scout Council that they had made a costly error when they let me sign up as a leader. I did not realize then, as I do now, that the Girl Scout Council would have let King Kong sign up as a leader. I did not realize that leaders were hard to get. I thought everyone was as eager as I was. It was when I was trying to find an assistant that I learned this.

And I took my responsibility seriously. I plunged into scouting with a vigor. The first thing I said every morning was "On My honor" . . . I was programmed. My husband thought it was fantastic. He especially liked the part where I would say "I will do my duty to God and my country." He thought he was God and our house the country. It was after he found out that I often volunteered his help in running the troop that his enthusiasm dimmed. He hauled hundreds of giggling Girl Scouts in our station wagon, clinched his teeth and never hit a one of them — not even once. I thought he behaved marvelously.

Meeting in the wintertime was the worst thing of all. It was bad. In fact, it was almost impossible. We couldn't meet outdoors when it snowed and it was nearly unthinkable indoors. The combination of damp wool coats, mittens and scarfs and a burning pot roast in the oven was like being stuck in a barn with a herd of noisy, wet sheep. I could hardly eat the treats they brought.

But they were the smells of life and Girl Scouting is Life with a capitol "L." It involves a lot of Living and Laughing and Loving . . .

And camping.

Unfortunately, it involves camping. Now, you all know how I feel about camping. It gives me stomach cramps.

But the Girl Scout Council sent out an edict. They proclaimed I could not conduct my troop's camp in an air-conditioned motel beside the swimming pool.

"How can you roast weiners and make muk-tuk stew on carpeting?" they asked.

"I'm not sure," I answered, "but Girl Scouts are supposed to be inventive. I'll find a way." I was positive I could.

However, I decided to be a good sport. I went camping just like everyone else. And I bought a pair of knee socks. Our son took one look at me in my knee socks and said I looked like an awful big fourth grader. My husband laughed. I rather liked them myself.

It is nice to know that Girl Scouts do not lose their femininity when they go to camp. Most of them take it right along with them. They love to squeal and act silly when they see a lizard and then if they think no one is looking, they like to pick it up and take it home and scare their mothers.

They complain about things like burned marshmallows and cleaning the latrine. They leave mirrors in the tents and burn holes in them and upset the lady in charge of council camping equipment. They gag over iodized water and then spend most of their camping days hanging over the water jug and they schedule tick hunts on each and are disappointed if they don't find one in their pigtails.

Adult camp leaders, counselors and directors develop strong headaches not curable by the ordinary first aid methods of aspirin and wet cloth. Personally, I have found that a cold beer after eight hours of day camp is almost as important as catching the bus in the morning.

The first two days of Girl Scout camp are really quite enjoyable. Camp mothers are fresh and bubbly. They do not have any mosquito bites, chigger bites, fever blisters, nor have they burned their fingerprints off the tips of their fingers by roasting them over reluctant campfires. They are enthusiastic.

The girls in the troop all have new slacks and T-shirts and they wear gaily colored scarfs on their heads without griping. They are 10 minutes early for the bus in the morning and loudly complain that it arrives too soon to take them home in the afternoon. They are anxious to explore just one more wooded area; find just one more perfect rock for the lodge "museum" and to stand at attention just one more time for flag ceremony. No one goes three inches from the group without a "buddy."

The camp director is cheerful, cooperative and smiles a lot. She is bustling and energetic, seeing to it that everyone is busy learning new songs and hustling to put campsites in order. At this point, scouts love assigned chores and fight over who will get the firewood.

By the third day the bus has to wait 10 minutes on the girls, one or two are left behind altogether and you can hear little envious snatches on the ride out to camp . . . "Lucky Gail. She has appendicitis and her mother wouldn't let her come to camp."

No one will sit with her assigned "buddy" on the bus. It is quite obvious they no longer believe in "togetherness" and possibly hope the other gets lost somewhere in the weeds. Or eaten by ticks!

It is also obvious that the camp mothers have turned into nags . . . Conversation centers around . . . "Put your scarfs back on girls . . . please, put your scarfs back on." Don't go barefoot, girls, please don't go barefoot," and "Girls, sing another song. Please, girls, sing another song!"

Only six small twigs of firewood have been gathered and everyone ate half-raw weiners for lunch. The troop is complaining of being hot, not wanting to hike anymore and that the latrine stinks. The camp director hasn't smiled all day.

On the fourth day of camp two or three of the mother's aren't speaking, the camp director will not even visit the campsites and is holed up in the lodge doing God only knows what and loud mutterings of "If I hear that stupid song one more time I'll stuff marshmallows down someone's throat," and "go bareheaded and get sunstroke, see if I care" rings through the bushes.

No one has gotten firewood at all and one leader makes the announcement that whoever wants to eat can just go get their own wood. Then she sits down under a tree and has a nice lunch of iced tea, lettuced tuna sandwiches, potato salad, jello and orange sherbet ice cream that her husband delivered, fresh and well-cooled, at the stroke of noon . . . and she doesn't share.

Very quietly, off in a corner, under the trees, you can hear another leader, chain-smoking and softly moaning, "Help me, Someone-please help me!"

She has assumed a prayerful position by a mulberry bush and you sort of know who she is calling on for help. He does not seem to hear her. He has avoided Girl Scout camp all week. He has no intentions of becoming anyone's "buddy."

Nearly 90 per cent of the girls in camp gather at the disembarkation point three hours early and four girls are placed at strategic points to shout "Here comes the bus!"

Small Brownies are nearly crushed in the stampede to board. The mothers always seem to get the best seats.

The girls in the troop all swear they won't even meet the bus the next day, they are quitting Girl Scouts first chance they get and if they have to wear those silly scarfs one more minute they will die . . . just die.

Camp is almost over!

The last day of camp is taunt with emotion. No one wants to leave. Little girls who have lived next door to each other for years are desperately clinging to one another, sobbing and swearing they will meet at camp again next year. They exchange blood-letting vows to be "buddies."

The leaders, too, have tears in their eyes and are clasping hands and hugging and promising to come back next year because it was such fun, the food was so good and they learned such nifty songs.

Sentiment hovers over the final flag ceremony like a thick mist. Someone starts to hum the strains of "Girl Scouts Forever" and there is some danger, for awhile, of one or two impressionable 13-year-olds fainting from the emotional impact of the whole scene.

The camp director still hasn't appeared since the third day but as the bus pulls slowly away from the camping area she can be seen, wistfully leaning against the door of the lodge waving her hand. Waving good-bye. She looks sad.

After a week at day camp I am emotionally drained, physically exhausted and covered with poison ivy. My husband keeps telling me I am not cut out to be a scout leader. But

I have a twisted personality — one that prefers most children to adults. And honestly, scouts are the greatest fun in the world . . . if you let them do all the work.

"WHY DO WE HAVE TO SEND GIRLS TO COLLEGE"

In this past two weeks or so I have harbored secret thoughts that it would be nice to have lived in the day and age when it was considered a waste to send a daughter to college.

Pioneer mothers certainly didn't have to suffer nerve pangs because of visions of educational merrymaking. They did sensible things with their daughters like skim milk, bake bread and crochet. They didn't send them a hundred miles from home to live in a dormitory. A coeducational dormitory! All they had to worry about was Indians and rattlesnakes. How peaceful it must have been to be a mother in the olden days!

It isn't that we are unexperienced parents as far as higher education is concerned. We sent our two sons to the university 10 checkbooks ago. They have been there long enough for us to be used to having them there. I thought I was prepared to send a daughter. So did my husband. So did our daughter.

"It's like Christmas in August," she called out gleefully, packing suitcase after suitcase with everything she owned.

The boys took a stuffed laundry bag and personalized beer mug and felt they were prepared to weather any storm. She was cleaning out her entire closet, her sister's closet and rummaging through mine.

"Just think," she said, "this is the last time I will sleep in this house as a civilian."

Was she going off to combat, I wondered? She seemed well adjusted to the fact she was leaving home. I was having a little trouble but, her whole being radiated confidence as we drove down the interstate.

She sat in front with her dad. I sat in the back with five suitcases, three tote bags, four boxes packed with what-nots, seven stuffed animals, a wardrobe bag, a typewriter, a bulletin board and a large, sturdy, shiny-green rubber plant.

"Now the first thing I want you to do," I advised, "is sign up for a karate class."

"Mother," she cried, filling the car with optimism, excitement challenge, change and bravado. "Don't be silly. I'll be fine!"

We were 10 minutes from home.

As we drew closer to the city she became quieter and the rubber plant began to droop.

"I'm a little bit scared," she admitted as we hit the inner-city traffic. "It is big and there are a lot of people."

She was right. There certainly were a lot of people and as luck would have it just as we pulled in front of her dorm we came face-to-face with a very strange male spirit, walking down the street dressed in a long, dingy gray, robe, back-pack perched on his shoulders, his hair flowing down his neck, sandals on his feet. He had an incredible look in his eye.

"Maybe that's my new roommate," our daughter joked. My husband definitely did not think that was funny. With a jerk of the steering wheel we whipped a U-turn in the middle of a crowd and headed in the other direction . . . toward home!

Of course we did not take her home. We had paid tuition and board and room. They were not going to give it back. It was let her stay or stay myself. And I knew right away that I didn't want to spend a night in that dormitory. Nor did the rubber plant. Its shiny green leaves turned pure white and its stalk reached out to me . . . pleadingly . . . begging to go back to its quiet corner in the living room by the television.

Four hundred stereos blared 400 different loud rock and roll songs through opened doors. The halls were crawling with noisy 18-year-olds. F.I.N.K. posters dominated the halls. I did not know what a F.I.N.K. was and I did not want to ask. Groaning elevators made trip after trip and I could not see any padlocked steel doors separating the boys' part from the girls' part anywhere.

Other parents wandered through the corridors with frightened, puzzled, lost looks in their eyes and on their faces. It was as if we had, at middle-age, been plunged into a youthful hell.

"Where will you study?" my husband asked, his ears automatically folding over his ear drums. "You can't study in all of this noise."

Our daughter smiled secretly as she eyed — she definitely eyed — three very tall, very broad-shouldered young freshmen boys as they galloped by her door. I think she was going to leave that studying worry up to mom and dad. I think she had other things to worry about. I think I did, too.

"Now, remember," I told her as we hugged her goodbye. "You don't have to stay here if you don't want to. Just call and we'll come and get you."

I bent down to the rubber plant . . . "You don't have to stay either," I whispered. I swear the soil trembled.

My husband and I stepped out into the bright outside. The sound of heavy traffic, squealing brakes, work whistles, diesel engines . . . the working city was like the hum of a lazy bee in comparison to the inside of the dormitory. We were safe! But was she?

She called the other night. "I love it," she thrilled. "It is great! I love my roommate, my teachers and my classes." She was bubbling. "And you should see my rubber plant. It's grown four inches."

Good grief, that silly plant likes college, I told my husband.

"And mom," she said, "want to know my favorite class?"

"Of course. What is it."

"Karate!"

Naturally, I'm worrying now why she took that particular class. She never takes my advice. I wonder if the rubber plant will tell.

"THE GINGERBREAD MYSTERY"

Now that school is really underway may I send out my congratulations . . . and a small amount of sympathy . . . to one earnest group of ladies known as room mothers. Personally, I have always wondered why they don't have room fathers. Let them take treats for awhile.

I am no longer classified as eligible to be a room mother. I am too old. I am very glad. This, perhaps, is one of the reasons I do not try to cover up the gray. I do not want anyone to make an error. I do not want anyone to think I might possibly qualify as a potential room mother. When I visit school I often stoop and walk slowly. I have no intentions of making any more gingerbread men.

You see that was my room mother specialty . . . and my room mother mistake. I started a tradition with our first child. At that time I thought the whole thing was adorable and great fun. And with only a few little cookie-cutters underfoot to distract me in the kitchen, I could bake with pleasure. I cleared the kitchen of poking fingers and flying feet, turned on soft music and created.

These were not your ordinary, plain, everyday men. These were gingerbread works of art. Productions. Originals. Creations. Not the common cookie molded out of plastic with a raisin stuck in its bellybutton. They were decorated and adorned.

I spent hours methodically applying tiny features on facial colored icing; drawing in eyebrows, eyelashes and pupils; little noses, rosebud mouths, rosy cheeks . . . and they were always smiling. Each had on a costume. Gay shirts and overalls —

buttons and bows. I wore out dozens of toothpicks and my eyes blurred. Our children, their classmates and the teacher loved them. I was hooked as the Gingerbread Lady for many years.

As the years went by, the classrooms grew. One of our daughters had 40 in her class. Unfortunately, 39 of them had smart mothers. This left me to be the room mother. And naturally our child asked for gingerbread men when the first treat time came up. Did I refuse? No! Did I falter? No! Did I cry? Yes!

And I transformed our kitchen into a gingerbread factory. Everywhere you turned little brown men in blue over-alls, white shirts, red suspenders and bright yellow buttons and shoes peered at you with wide eyes. The house was crawling with them. A sickening sweet smell hung over the furniture.

"How much longer are we going to have to live with grinning gingerbread?" my husband asked, fanning the front door to clear the air.

"Not much longer," I sighed. "I'm packing them for school right now."

Augie-Doggie and our youngest son watched in fascination as I neatly put the little dears in a big, white box . . . layer by layer, tissue-in-between. The box had the label of the town's best store on it. These fellows were going first class. And as I fell into bed that night the hungry eyes of Augie-Doggie and our youngest son eventually were replaced by dreams of shortening and All-Spice. I slept well. I was tired.

Our daughter was very proud as she prepared to go to school the next morning. She promised to carry the box with tenderness and not to stub her toe.

"Let me take one last look," I said as she started out the door. I wanted to say goodbye. I peeped inside the box.

Three of the Gingerbread Men had been murdered! Their mutilated bodies stared back at me. A head was missing on one — an arm and a leg on another one — one had lost his entire torso. I did not have to search far to find who had committed the crime. Hungry eyes had given them away. They might as well have had a foot sticking out of their mouths. Dog and son had done it. They were convicted. They were guilty.

I soothed our daughter's tears and repeated over and over to myself . . . "Mothers cannot beat up on dogs and babies!" But she CAN sit them on the couch and tell them to stay there until she tells them they can move. I thought seriously of letting both sit until they were 72 years old!

"Just tell the teacher that you don't want one," I told our daughter, "and tell the teacher she doesn't want one and hope that one of your classmates is absent!"

As it turned out two or three of the children in the class were absent and there was enough for each to have one . . . including the teacher.

She called me later. We talked about gingerbread men. She said the children loved them. She said she liked hers, too.

In fact, she told me, she liked her so well she had planned to preserve it. For posterity or her coffee break . . . she didn't say why . . . but she did say that the gingerbread man remained on her desk throughout the school day and that each time she left the room and returned the gingerbread man became smaller and smaller — bite by bite. He was gradually nibbled to death. I knew it was not Augie-Doggie or our son who had wickedly assassinated the teacher's cookie. I had them safe at home all day — on the couch. Some other sweet tooth had chewed it. Poor teacher, all she had left at the end of the day was a big, bright, yellow button.

There must be a moral to this story somewhere . . . and the only one I can think of is . . .

"Put everything you don't want eaten by kids — and dogs — up very, very high."

STIFLING CLEANING IMPULSES

Every ounce and toil and labor at our house has been directed to outdoor living. The lawn and garden don't look bad . . . it is inside the house where the weeds are growing.

Little spiders merrily make their webs cozy and comfortable for summer living. They have set up vacation homes in the corner of the dining room. A newspaper has taken root under the coffee table. Gum wrappers bloom in perfect profusion behind the couch; the sweet scent of ripe tube socks permeates the air; dust nodules dip and sway in the evening breeze and the carpet is freshly sodded with junk.

Oh, how I wish someone would invent a riding vacuum cleaner.

"I really think the house could use a good spring cleaning," my husband suggested recently. "After all, June is just around the corner. Soon it will be too late. Perhaps you would like to borrow my rototiller," he added, plowing trash from his favorite chair.

"What a dandy suggestion," I smiled sweetly, making poison-gestures behind his back, "I will start by throwing things away."

He nodded in agreement. "I will start with your side of the closet," I said.

He swayed with shock. Running to our bedroom he crushed himself against the closet door. "Stop!" he shouted. He was sweating. "Do not do anything foolish."

I hadn't intended to. All I wanted to do was get rid of the shirts he wore every day. The shirts with the buttons hanging by a slender thread; the shirts with pockets torn and weeping on his chest; the ones with the bright patterns faded and washed away; the ones with the wrinkled armpits. These were his favorite shirts. These were the ones that screamed for the gentle and tender touch of a good wife. These were the ones he chose to wear in public. I don't know why he did that.

Possessively he gathered them to his bosom. I would have to wrench his arm off to get them away from him. I didn't want to do that. I turned to other things. I would let him keep his shirts.

"Why do you still keep this old pair of trousers?" I asked, holding up a glum looking piece of brown corduroy material held together by a broken zipper. "I think I will just put them in the Goodwill box, but heaven knows what they will do with them. I think if they are washed one more time they will dissolve." I shook my head in sad disbelief.

"Well, don't wash them," he answered testily, snatching the brown mess from my hands and adding them quickly to the shirts he still clutched under his arm. "They are my garden pants. They are comfortable. They are like old friends. You do not donate old friends to the Goodwill."

Well, I can think of a few . . . but then we won't go into that.

I had bombed out on shirt and pants. I tried for shoes. This was a real mess. Tangled in a stew of shoestrings were a dozen pair of shoes . . . assorted in color, style and state of disrepair.

"Now take this old pair of cowboy boots," I said holding one up in review. "There is no way you can wear this pair of boots."

I demonstrated by pointing out a broken tongue, an injured instep and a cracked sole. "Why, these things are disgraceful."

His face blanched. I thought he was going to have a stroke. I quickly moved a small chair behind him in case he fainted. I didn't want him to crack his head on the woodwork. He might have a messy wardrobe but I didn't want him hurt, after all.

"My God!" he cried. "I have just broken them in good. Do you realize how long it takes to break in a pair of good boots? A lifetime of sore feet. I can wear those now without flinching and you want to take them away from me." I thought he was going to cry.

I was a witch. I had desecrated a shrine. I was not sorry. I kept on. I may be fat but I'm not dumb.

"Now, let's just move on," I said, patting him lovingly on the cheek. "Let's just see what we have up here on the shelf.

Surely some of this can be thrown away."

I reached for the top of the shelf. A steel-like grip came down on my wrist like a vise.

"There's nothing up there to be thrown away," he growled. The tips of his ears were turning white. I was trodding on dangerous and forbidden territory. Quite truthfully, I knew all along there was nothing up there but I was just about to reach my goal. He was about to give in. My "good, little, tidy housewife" efforts were going to pay off . . . I just knew they were.

"Oh, hey there," he smiled, releasing my wrist and caressing my shoulder. The color came back to his face. "Let's forget all this cleaning nonsense and go to town. I'll let you use credit cards wherever and whenever you want. Why, I'll even take you out for dinner. How's that!"

Triumphantly I closed the closet door on the sad shirts, the pathetic pants and the battered boots . . . I was safe for another year!

I did not have to spring clean after all!

IT'S NICE TO BE MISSED AT HOME

It would be, oh so nice, to be considered indispensable. It would be so nice to have my children and husband sit by the front door, hands folded humbly, eyes downcast, tears flowing with strained looks on their faces, anxiously awaiting my return after a three or four day absence.

Actually, Augie-Doggie DOES sit by the front door with a humble and strained look on his face but it isn't because he is waiting for me. He has his own problems.

I have always wanted to believe that when I am gone the entire household ceases to function. I would also like to believe that my husband wears black pajamas and mourns my empty side of the bed. I don't think he does.

I would like to think that our children are so saddened by my not being there they do not talk on the telephone, play the stereo or watch violence on TV. I don't think it matters.

"You aren't being realistic, Mom," our son commented as he passed the refrigerator and genuflected. "We will miss you but we aren't going to fall apart. We are independent. After all, isn't that what a parent strives for . . . independency in their children?"

He is right, of course, but why, I wondered, is there no evidence of independence when I am home? When, then, am I the

91

only one in the house that knows how to work a toilet paper spindle? It isn't that I haven't given lessons. I have. I have stopped the children at their play, my husband from his nap and called in Augie-Doggie from outside.

"Come," I said, "we are all going to learn a new skill. We are going to learn how to replace the toilet paper spindle when it becomes empty. It will be fun and educational. We will learn two different methods of placing the paper properly. You can take your pick. I do not care in which direction it rolls. I just care that it rolls."

Everyone groaned . . . and mumbled and complained. They did not sound one bit independent to me.

"Pay attention!" I reminded. "I'm going to give grades." Everyone flunked.

They also flunked cleaning the oven, shaking throw rugs, straightening curtains, replacing toothpaste caps, vacuuming under chairs, dusting the television screen, cleaning light fixtures, updating the calendar, polishing faucets, washing the coffee pot, picking up shoes, hanging up jackets and filling salt shakers.

"My God," I cried, "I can't leave. You'll all evaporate from neglect. How can you manage without me?"

"Go!" my husband commanded. "We'll be fine. We can manage."

It didn't help matters when I looked into his eyes and saw he didn't even seem sad. In fact, if the truth were known, he seemed quite cheerful. So did the children. Augie-Doggie was the only one that even tried to look sorrowful. He knows what side his dog food is buttered on, that old dog does.

I took one last look as the car rounded the corner. "Goodbye, dear house," I sobbed. "You will probably be a crumbled bit of dust, buried in toilet paper, when I return."

"Goodbye dear children. You will probably be starved, little independent skeletons when I return."

"Goodbye, dear husband. You will probably be a wilted and withered lonely old man with a broken heart when I return."

I really didn't enjoy my visit. And it was made less pleasant by the fact when I called home things seemed so stable. I heard no screaming in the background. I heard no one yelling at anyone. I heard no highpitched voice giving commands to "Get those dishes done . . . clean up that mess . . . get at your homework . . . you cannot go downtown . . . who took my lipstick . . . and for goodness sakes pick up this bathroom!"

A voice was missing in that household. A voice I recognized. A voice I had with me.

When the voice and I finally did return home I expected the worst. It was with some surprise that I noticed the house was still standing. It looked crystal-like in its peaceful setting. The shrubs even looked chubbier.

The children burst from the door. They were glowing in good health. Tanned (in the winter-time?), wholesome, full of nutritious independence.

My husband's footsteps were light. He did not look like a man who had been lanquishing for anyone — for anything.

I stepped into a palace. Everything was squeaky clean. Even the oven. A full roll of paper blessed the spindle. It might have had exclamation marks around it, it was so obvious. Curtains were hanging delicately from the rods, there were no gnats in the light fixtures, no dishes in the sink or no jackets on the floor. Everything looked great. My ego was definitely bruised.

And then I noticed Augie-Doggie. He was guarding the utility room door. He tried to attack me when I put my hand on the doorknob. His heart wasn't in it.

"Down, boy," I said. "You are no killer."

I opened the door. And there I saw the first mountain I had seen since our trip to Colorado. It was a varied colored and textured mountain of denim, cotton, polyester, knits, terry cloth and nylon. Not one soul had washed one load while I was gone. A grateful happy, sob rose in my throat. I was happy.

They missed me after all.

THE CALL OF THE WILD

I certainly don't have to tell you how I feel about family camping. I have never tried to hide the fact my family is the outdoor type. Nor have I tried to hide the fact I am the indoor, sit in an easy chair, read a good book and sip a cool drink type.

But they have always outnumbered me eight to one and any way you look at it, over the ironing board, around the kitchen, changing the sheets or mending socks, those are pretty big odds. They are also pretty big odds when it comes time to take a vacation.

Every year I continue to vote for an air-conditioned motel near a large shopping center and spending the remainder of our vacation funds on theatre tickets, babysitters, meals outside the home and beauty parlor appointments. My husband votes to go camping.

And because he is bigger than I am, richer than I am and the only one in the family allowed to drive our car out of the city limits, the children vote along with him and there it is again... eight to one.

A few years ago, after the usual yearly farce of letting mother cast her silly vote, the rest of them picked the spot where we would camp. They chose a Nebraska state lake about 90 miles from home.

Now if it had to be camping this particular lake was not so bad. It was close to civilization, surrounded by lovely trees, the water was shallow enough for safe swimming, the beaches were sandy and the fishing was good.

We were even frivolous enough to make plans to spend the weekend with some friends at their newly purchased lot. They had just bought it and were eager to show it off. I envied them the long, low trailer equipped with electricity, hot and cold running water, a REAL bathroom with chrome, and soft, squishy beds. I growled a lot as we erected our tent some 50 feet away.

Two more families joined us and we spent the weekend roasting corn in the sand, rescuing small children who drifted too far in their inner tubes, chasing the gulls that landed in droves on the island across the beach and playing a little bridge.

"If I have to camp," I thought, "this isn't half bad."

Then the weekend was over and our friends packed their pots and pans, their campers and their wet bathing suits and took off for home and "the daily grind." These were my husband's words . . . not mine. He really and truly felt sorry for them. I didn't. I felt sorry for myself. Two days in a tent was my smiling limit. My mouth corners were beginning to droop.

Our affluent friends with the trailer had offered us the keys and the use of the beautiful and comfortable thing while we were there, but my husband drew himself up in proud virility and turned them down — flat. After all, he was a tent man. I took the keys, pride be hanged and promised that we wouldn't take advantage of their hospitality unless an emergency came up. It did. You knew it would. It always does.

The next day dawned clear and windy. We paddled around in the water, drove into town for supplies and to see live people, toured the island and settled a few family quarrels. About six o'clock that evening it began to drizzle. This didn't surprise me. It always rains when we pitch our tent. I've learned to accept this along with charcoaled rice krispies for breakfast and brushing my teeth in public.

We sat on the dock and fished in the rain for awhile. This isn't my idea of a fun-filled evening but it beats being stuck in an airtight tent with nothing but the pitter-patter of rain on canvas for entertainment. I won't let anyone bring a Coleman lantern inside and there certainly aren't too many things a family of nine can do in a dark tent.

Finally, after being thoroughly dampened and chilled to the bone, I drew in my fishing line, tossed a surly "the heck with it" over my shoulder, plodded up the path to the tent and cast a grudging eye at the fabulous trailer that was just sitting there, lonely and unloved. I loved it . . . but none of the rest of my nature-worshipping family gave it a second thought.

We were all in bed at 8 p.m. At home when I suggest bedtime at 8, I have a near riot on my hands and our children do everything to gun me down with excuses and complaints. But in the damp woods there wasn't a heck of a lot they could do about it. No television, no light to read by and the transistor was so full of snap, crackles and pops we couldn't even hear the weather report. But we really didn't have to hear a report of the weather. We were in a position to know first-hand just what was going on in that great weather station in the sky.

When you are stuck in a tent on a lake and have no way to communicate with the outside world and have a radio that carried nothing in its tubes but static, the only way to determine the condition of the weather is to look outside the tent. I did and boy, was I shocked.

We were right in the middle of a rain storm . . . a wind storm . . . a thunder storm . . . a lightning storm . . . In fact, I wouldn't have been surprised to see a blizzard come up over the horizon. The weather was doing everything else. Thunder rolled over the lake. By the time it reached our tent it built itself up into one giant boom Boom BOOM! Loud, crashing and terrifying.

I was scared to death. My cot vibrated with electric shocks as the lightning slipped in beneath the tent. One of the children complained of drowning in a puddle of water that had crept in beneath the sleeping bag and two or three others were huddled like kapok cocoons in a corner. My husband told us it would soon pass over, to relax, it was just a little summer storm and there was certainly nothing to be afraid of. He lied.

The thunder and lightning continued and it grew in ferocity until I thought my whole body would disintegrate from nerve shock.

It was now about one in the morning. The "little summer storm" had been going on for four hours and was showing absolutely no signs of wanting to crawl back under the clouds and go to sleep. I had reached the fine edge of hysteria and the drowning child was gurgling and the cocoons had been joined by three others. Everyone was herded into one corner and miserable. Even my husband had stopped his cheerful little banter and had said some very bad words once or twice.

Suddenly, someone up there in charge of things, put his shoulder to the wheel and put together the biggest mass of noise in the world, the brightest streak of electricity and all the smoke and fire he could muster, molded them into one hunk and hurled it down on top of our tent. The world split apart and our canvas tent rocked.

"O-Kay. That's it!" my husbans shouted, his hitherto courageous camping face ashen. "Let's go to the trailer."

I was up, out and in the door before he could possibly change his mind. Eight bodies crowded in behind me.

"Where are my mighty campers now?" I thought. Scared . . . just like I was!

It was lovely in the trailer. Electricity blazed through the inside like sunrise on Easter morning. The walls muffled the thunder and we drew the drapes against the bright lightning. It was so snug and peaceful.

I brewed coffee and everyone, even the little children, had a sip or two. The outside world and its miseries seemed a thousand miles away. We were safe! Let it storm. It couldn't get me — or my loved ones. Even my husband had to admit this beat drowning.

Everyone found a comfortable, dry bed and we turned out the lights and settled down to finish what was left of a very short night.

I had barely adjusted my pillow for the last time, called out the final goodnight and blessed our trailer owning friends in prayer for the hundredth time when I heard strange voices outside our window. Strange men's voices.

"Do you think there is anyone in there?" one voice said . . . deep, low and menacing.

"I don't know!" said another in a much deeper, much lower and much more menacing voice. An eerie flashlight beam played along the sides of the trailer.

"Oh, God," I thought, "we'll all be killed and robbed in our sleep."

Mind you, it was still thundering and no one could have heard the trumpeting of an elephant herd, let alone the screams of a suffering woman.

I could see the headlines in The Independent. "Family Wiped Out In Camping Massacre. Mother Slain While Being Good Sport."

I knew I had been right. I knew we should never have come. I told them so. I told them we would have been safer in a city surrounded by smog and muggers. But they wouldn't listen. They never do. And now we were all going to be ravished.

The "Voices" started beating on the sides of the trailer with heavy (and I was convinced murderous) fists. I searched for a weapon. The only thing I could find was a fingernail file. It wasn't going to help a whole lot.

"Who is there?" I shouted in my deepest, most masculine voice.

My husband was fumbling around in a confined space trying to put on his pants, more concerned with preserving his modesty than his life. I was in my nightgown and couldn't have cared less.

For years I had tried to convince my family into agreeing with me that camping was dangerous.

I had always told them we were treading the edge of terror everytime we pitched the tent in the woods. I had always told them that I was not being foolish because I slept with an ax under my pillow.

Oh, how I wished for that ax the night the strangers approached our friend's trailer. So did my husband.

"Where's your ax?" he whispered as the "voices" continued to pound desperately on the outside of the trailer.

"I left it in the tent!" I whispered back. I wanted to say "I told you so" but I didn't. I didn't really want the last words we might possibly say to each other to sound pithy. I didn't want to enter eternity with cross words between us.

Besides I was concerned about the children. Why, the poor little things must be terrified. My husband and I must pull ourselves together, I thought. After all, we are supposed to be the guiding adult factors in the family. They musn't see how frightened we were. We must be calm and soothe them in their fear. I could imagine just how horrified they must be.

I was wrong. One of them had gotten up and quietly opened the door to the strangers while their father and I huddled in the bedroom discussing the ax.

We found our visitors were not threats to our lives but two very nice gentlemen who had come through the rain to warn us that there was one heck of a cabin fire up the line and that we should get out of the trailer . . . fast. They didn't have to speak more than once.

We got out . . . FAST! Little pajamaed bodies peeled out of that trailer like bullets. The "Voices" stood by in stunned amazement at the hornet's nest they had stirred up. I don't think they were quite prepared for mass rescue.

I was the last one out — still dressed sensually in my nightdress. I camp beautifully. I gave one, last calm look around the trailer and picked out the things I thought needed saving.

I took one feather pillow, one talking Drowsy doll, and one blue canvas tote which contained deodorant, toothpaste, shaving lotion and a box of baggies.

I left my purse, my watch, the camera, my housecoat and our youngest child.

My husband went back for our child. He also got my ax from the tent. "Just in case," he said sheepishly. "Thank you, Lord!" I said quietly. "Maybe they will listen to me from now on." They haven't.

We all flocked to the station wagon to watch what would happen next. It was the only place we had to go. It was very hot and humid in the car with the windows all rolled up and baggies are poor substitutes for tissue papers when it comes to wiping off perspiration. I told them all to quit complaining . . . didn't I bring the deodorant! Besides we were safe and that's all that mattered.

The cabin, a few lots up from our spot, was soaring to the skies in flames, smoke and parks. It couldn't possibly be saved. I had known all along that the bolt that had driven us from the tent had a double whammy attached and the poor burning cabin proved it.

It was a terrible and ghastly sight and each one of the children solemnly swore he would never, never play with matches. Smokey the Bear got some new recruits that night, believe me. It ran through my mind that I might stop smoking but I was much too nervous.

We were limp with relief when we heard the sound of fire engines wailing over the hills. We shouted and clapped our hands like kids at the circus. One or two of the children were relaxed enough in the back seat to make sly comments like . . . "Mom sure does look funny sitting in the car in her nightgown."

We watched the firemen battle the fire and put it out. The heavy rain had saved the trees, thus sparing the surrounding cabins, our friends trailer and unfortunately our tent.

I had tried to mentally guide a spark or two toward the tent but they just fell around it, lay on the ground and sputtered out.

Our tent was still complete, intact, and stood leering at me. It stood there as if to say . . . "you tried — didn't you honey! You tried to get rid of me. But you won't. I'll be around for a long time to go on vacation with you. It will take more than a silly little old electrical storm to get rid of me."

And it was right. It is still around. But someday I'll get it. You wait and see. Who knows . . . I may do it in this summer.

ROOM FOR IMPROVEMENT

If reservations are needed to cement a place in heaven I know some husbands who aren't going to make it.

They will wander from cloud-to-cloud to find a final resting place. It could take them centuries of sky hopping and then they might have to curl up in their sleeping bags on a spare star.

Most of them, I think, would rather do that anyway rather than admit they might have to call in advance.

Under most circumstances my husband is a pre-planner.

Next spring's seeds have been ordered, the snow shovel is polished and hung in an easy-to-reach place, a tidy supply of fuses are labeled with room numbers, mouse traps are readied for the first frost rush, credit cards are in alphabetical order for Christmas, a miniature computer stands by for the first of the month bills, tire rotation dates are set up on the calendar, postage stamps are pre-moistened and his last will and testament is in good shape. The man is definitely organized.

And he personally prepares well for a trip — even an overnighter. We never run out of gas, he knows our CB call letters backward, he has checked for holes in his socks, his comb is clean and well sifted and his toothbrush is packed, soldier stiff and at attention. Nothing is left to chance. Everything is ready.

Except — and it is a large, looming, loathsome except — we have no place to spend the night. We never have any place to spend the night. Ten seconds and a wats line could bring us a deluxe motel room ... but my husband, my well-organized, methodical, established pillar of a husband does not believe in making reservations.

This is a flaw in his character. The flaw in MY character reminds him of this as we head down the Interstate.

"Did you make reservations?" I ask, my nerve ends curling in anticipation. I know what his answer will be. I like to suffer. "Not necessary!" he answers swinging by a semi within suction distance.

"Where will we stay?" I persist ... visions of deluxe zooming down to decay.

"We will find a place!" he grits. "We always do!"

And he is right ... we always do find a place ... but in the process a rugged and vigorous rip is made in the harmony of our marriage.

It is hard for me to accept the sudden change in my husband's habits. Ordinarily, he tells me it is wicked and wasteful to drive two blocks out of the way to save $1.59 on a pantyhose sale. But here he is, whipping around Nebraska's largest city 52 times searching for a "No Vacancy" sign.

By the time we find it I am hungry, tired, weak, sweaty, frustrated, nervous, very cross and I usually have to go to the bathroom ... bad!

He continues to be optimistic and zig-zags through the city, darting in-and-out of motel offices. He pays very little attention to the lady writhing in agony beside him. He forges happily on, just as if the little god of motel registrars rides at his elbow. The rip in our marriage is widening.

But one time ... one time ... the little god turncoated and sat on my lap. It was memorable. And not too long ago. It had to do with his philosophy that motels on the outskirts of any populated place were hoping for tenants — and that hopeful

99

motels were cheaper than any other kind.

Block by block we searched the perimeter of the city. Hundreds of husbands had gotten there before us. There wasn't a motel to be found anywhere. It was drawing close to checkout time and we hadn't even checked in!

Each turn around the city brought us closer and closer to the shining tower of the most expensive and exclusive motel in the area. It was so expensive and exclusive it didn't bother with occupancy signs. It dared you to inquire. The little god on my lap gleefully leaped with joy as my husband pulled in under the glamorous canopy.

He came back with a key in trembling hand. We had a room for the night. An expensive room. A room that cost $42.50. For two!

It was deluxe all right. Spacious, with plush carpeting, a chandelier, mirrored wall, tasteful interior, in-room movies, vibrating king-sized bed, gaily colored toilet paper . . . it was DELUXE. I loved every inch of it.

I glanced over and saw my husband with his head sadly bent. Small shiny tears were running down his cheeks as he tucked his now-slim billfold into our suitcase. He was mumbling something about putting lumps on a little god's head.

"You're right," he said, defeat weighing each syllable. "We should have had reservations."

"Don't be silly," I smiled. "Who needs to call ahead?"

Personally, I love surprises. Especially when they are expensive!

MIXED RESULTS IN THE GARDEN

I am nearly certain that some people crawl around on their hands and knees, manicuring their lawns with tweezers as diligently and carefully as I pluck my eyebrows.

How else can every blade of grass be as even as the skyline . . . with no patches in between?

And GREEN! Why, I know they must run out after the sun goes down and spray paint. Grass is grass, as I see it . . . and I see ours as being lime-colored, with splotches of light brown and dead yellow.

Recently I borrowed my husband's overalls, bought a straw hat down town and picked a piece of straw from our archery bale. Clutching this between my teeth I surveyed our land. It didn't look good. It could be the dog, I decided.

But then I can't justify blaming everything on Augie-Doggie. Augie doesn't bat a golf ball about or play jump rope in the petunias or ride a bike through the hedge or let an inner tube coagulate in the center of the lawn all summer. He might have an occasional vice but he doesn't stomp around.

And it wasn't lack of fertilizer. We use fertilizer — lots of it. It makes the dandelions grow as strong as oaks. Some of them even have acorns. Fuzz balls whip and dance all over our yard, dropping their tiny weed seeds in abandoned bliss.

My husband suggested I plant flowers if I didn't like the way things looked. I don't know why he suggested I plant flowers. He knows that my tulips are the only ones in the world that grow sitting down — and that I raise beige roses ... with black tips. They even smell funny. I can doom a hollyhock to a sudden, twitching death by just opening the packet of seeds.

Don't get me wrong. I admire those women who have the time and ability to poke around in the soil and grow things. But I get all the soil I want in the children's closet. I certainly don't have to commune with nature in order to get the earthy contact. However, considering the condition of our lawn and the level of my complaints, I decided to do my best to improve the situation. I would have a flower garden.

I dreamed of running around in a profusion of multicolored flowers in a white, wide-brimmed hat, polka dotted Swiss dress, carrying a pale blue watering can ... sort of like Marueen O'Hara in the movies, dancing on tippy-toe through the dahlias.

In reality I looked more like Ma Kettle in the thistles.

I knew right away buying packets of seeds would be a big mistake. There is no way that I can identify the flower from the weed when they start to sprout. I hated to think of spending an entire summer crouched down cultivating sheep sorrel and poison ivy. I bought pre-bedded plants. And I bought a book. It had 900 pages of everything the gardener needs to know.

I read the first page and knew I was in deep trouble. I did not know the difference between an annual and a perennial; an anemone and a zinnia; brown rot from broadleaf, or an Asiatic garden beetle from a cutworm. And I didn't particularly care, especially about the beetle and the worm.

I do not like crawling creatures of any type ... be they garden or garage-flower or floor. I was almost positive I might meet up with some if I planted a garden. And I did.

And I met up with other problems while burrowing in the dirt with my bare hands. I called our youngest daughter ...

"Please keep your kitty out of my garden patch!"

I was very serious. I was also very nauseated.

My husband asked me why I was planting alyssum with my

nose wrinkled.

I told him about the kitty.

"Dirt is dirt," he said. "You have to take the bad with the good. Your attitude is all wrong about this whole thing."

Well, all I know is, the book didn't say a thing about attitude. And it didn't say anything about little potted plants that wither and fade the minute they are thrust into the ground . . . and it didn't say a thing about spreading kitty litter between the buttercups . . . and it didn't mention four o'clocks that don't know what time it is . . . and it didn't say anything concerning the morning glory that only blossoms after dark.

It did tell me the difference between a hoe and a rake — and how to use them. I have that down pat.

So far, the only thing that has bloomed are my blisters. They look wonderful!

"GARDEN CREATIONS"

Well, we had that garden again this year. But this year, we (I say "we" but actually it was "him") were creative.

Our neighbors had gardens thick with great jungles of rhubarb, sweet corn, peas, beans, cucumbers, tomatoes and juicy bermudas. We grew herbs. We had masses of basil, marjoram, rosemary, caraway, dill and fennel meandering around our garden patch like hobgoblins . . . none of them stayed where we drilled the hole and planted the seed. They changed beds as often as some of the swingier people we know are reputed to do.

But they thrived, and once I got used to distinguishing the herbs from the weeds and could be sure I was not dressing up a dinner salad with ragweed instead of Sweet Basil, I was home free.

My husband was an expert at picking between an herb and a weed but I often had a little trouble. I could recognize foxtails and Russian thistles with no problem. I knew they weren't herbs. I'm not that dumb. But after he caught me tearing up tiny seedlings by the roots (an incident he still refers to in witty conversations as "The Rape of Rosemary") he assigned me to the potato patch.

"Hardly anyone can kill a potato plant," he told me. Well, I tried. Believe me, I tried. There's nothing uglier than a potato plant. Actually, there's nothing to it at all. It just sits there and grows and grows. All over the place. I tried raising a few flowers in between to pep up the potatoes, but they all got some sort of disease and instead of waxing straight and tall and colorful they hunched up in weak little bunches, and like tiny earthangels begging someone to relieve them of the awful burden of blooming, they turned meager blossoms heavenward and . . . died. One by one.

The potato plants grew strong and tall and thick and green and just shoved those poor little flowers right in the ground.

"Why do you hate the potato plants so?" my husband asked, coming into the house with a grubby bucket full of very muddy, dirty, misshapen potatoes.

"This is why I hate potato plants," I answered, taking the bucket from his hands. "I do not like to cook with potatoes that are dirty, muddy and misshapen. I like to cook with potatoes that are round and white and clean and come in plastic bags from the grocery store."

"But these are cheaper," he answered.

And I suppose they are. "But cheaper is not always better," I said.

We have this discussion often . . . and it is not always about potatoes. And I very seldom win.

I didn't win about the cucumbers either. Now, I do like cucumbers. In fact, very often I do not wait for cucumbers to grow in our garden. I will buy them in the store when they are out-of-season and expensive. I do not get tired of cucumbers. I eat them raw, with vinegar and sugar and on peanut butter sandwiches. I eat a lot of cucumbers and enjoy every bite.

But I did not want to make pickles out of them. Here again, we had the cheaper vs. better discussion.

"I can not see where my making pickles will save any money," I discussed. "You do realize that I can take a very firm, straight, green cucumber and turn it into a soft, squishy, yellow pickle that no one will eat. I have done this before and more than likely will do it again."

"Follow the recipe," he advised, ending the discussion and handing me the grubby bucket full of very firm, straight, green cucumbers. He also handed me a recipe. It was called "Thunder and Lightning Pickles."

He was truly intuitive. For as I worked in the steamy kitchen . . . it "thundered and lightninged." Not outside. Oh no, not outside . . . but over the stove, in the kitchen, while I was boiling jars and mixing brine . . . my temper thundered and my vocabulary spouted lightning.

And the very firm, straight, green cucumbers turned to soft, squishy, yellow pickles that no one would eat . . . right before my eyes.

My husband said it was my attitude. I still say those cucumbers were smart . . . they knew all along that cheaper is not always better.

BECOMING BEAUTIFUL AT HOME

Beauty secrets have always failed me. I am a classic "before." Just once before I depart this earth I would like to be classified an "after." That is why I joined the monthly cosmetic club.

My family reacted with detachment. They didn't take it seriously. Just another one of mother's whims. It will never last, they thought, the first day I received my kit and went to work applying the eyeliners, creams, blushes, moisturizers, etc. Our youngest daughter crouched in the corner waiting for me to lose interest so she could claim the leftovers and be the only seventh grader to enter junior high with 'cel pour les levres" lips. I told her not to get her hopes up.

As the days passed it was obvious things weren't shaping up as they were supposed to. The ladies in the illustrations turned into beautiful goddesses of seduction following application. I still looked like a piece of beef jerky. I kept trying.

"This should do it," I muttered to myself, lifting a tube of ice-mint peel-off masque from my kit. The instructions said it was what nature had intended.

"Good," I thought. "Nature knows!"

What nature didn't know, however, was that I have a terrible time following directions. I lose interest with details, my mind wanders and I'm apt to overlook important steps ... such as the time limit for leaving on facial masques.

I spread it generously over my face, just as the instructions said ... perhaps a little too generously, now that I look back on it. I included my throat but avoided my eyelids. Inadvertently I enclosed my eyebrows and the gel oozed into my hairline. "Oh well," I thought, "the edges are just as important as the surface. If I'm going to do this I might as well do it right and go all the way." I left it dripping from my earlobes.

I danced into the living room. My masque was taking effect. My throat was closing.

"Why is your face all screwed up?" our son asked. "Your eyebrows are stretching."

I ignored him. True, my earlobes were beginning to tighten, the corners of my mouth felt like rubber bands, my nostrils were spreading at an alarming rate. In fact, I was a little concerned that my facial features were going to pop right out and roll across the carpet. The cat was licking her lips. She is very alert when things go skittering pell-mell across the floor.

I was supposed to leave it on for 15 to 20 minutes. There was little doubt in my mind this time limit applied to the young-and-the-beautiful. For the old-and-the-gray a good 30 to 45 minutes should do it up nicely. So I sat there. My face stretching.

The family turned off the television and watched as my eyebrows lost their arch. The only thing I could move by now was my eyelids. I fluttered them to let everyone know I was still alive. I had long ago eliminated the power of speech. You can't talk with a constricted throat and a pursed mouth the size of a cherry pit. And I will have to admit it was an uncomfortable situation. My husband was finding it all very entertaining.

The time was finally up. It had turned into a very long three-quarters of an hour. The directions said "Masque should peel off easily." Good, I thought. "IF" (could this mean trouble?) it doesn't peel easily — remove with special "Easy Take-It-Off."

There was trouble. No doubt about it. Someone had failed to include "Easy Take-It-Off" in my kit. I looked for it. It definitely wasn't there. I started to peel.

My God, the stuff was stuck!! I couldn't budge it. It was on there like concrete. My face was becoming stiffer and stiffer. I was getting scared.

My family crowded into the bathroom to watch. The cat sat in the bathtub, twitching her tail and grinning.

"Use your fingernail to lift the edge," our daughter suggested. I do not have fingernails.

"Try some cold cream," another said. The cold cream slithered down my cheek and landed in a heap on my foot.

"How about sandpaper?" my husband giggled. He was enjoying this very, very much. I scratched and clawed at my face. I lifted a little edge. With one big peel I began taking the masque from my face . . . with it came my hairline and my eyebrows. What pain! I thought for a minute that I would have no lips left.

"There goes any kissing I had in mind," I whimpered. Tendrils of paper-thin, plastic-like substance hung from my nose and ears. I looked so very bad. I didn't have the healthy-looking glow I had been promised. Not at all. Later, my ego and face splotched and stewed, I sobbed through tensed mouth to my husband . . . "I'll never be beautiful! Never, never, never!"

"That's OK," he said softly nibbling on my red-hot earlobe, "you just be you. That's beautiful enough for me."

They don't sell that in a kit, believe me.

PLANNING CHILDREN'S CAREERS

My husband and I are of the opinion that our children are exceptional. Now and then we notice a flaw . . . and once in a while the flaw resembles a gash . . . but on the whole and most of the time they are very satisfactory.

Naturally, we are interested in them . . . their dreams, their ambitions, their careers . . . their futures. I wonder what they will do with their lives?

Personally, I think they should ask their mother.

I have not spent the last 25 years in a paper sack, you know. I have observed, watched and listened. I think I know what they do best.

One, for instance, would make a whale of a telephone operator. She was born with a dial tone . . . and she has not relinquished her birthright. The telephone is her past, her present and her future. I am sure when she goes to heaven she will be the only angel there whose wing tips give out busy signals.

I have no trouble finding this child when I want her to clean her room. I just follow the telephone cord. It's a dead give-away. I speak to her in area code and she understands. Looking back, I suspect I marked her before she was born. My husband claims she takes after me. I suppose she does. For a long time the telephone was the only thing that held any mystery in my life. I knew what I'd find when I changed a diaper or swept behind the refrigerator but you never know who or what is on the other end of the telephone when it rings. I understand her interest. I truly do. Maybe it will be her career.

More than likely, one will rub noses with royalty. She is a self-appointed princess. She has always thought of herself as a fairy child . . . living in a world of Rose Reds and Snow Whites, waiting for the charming prince to come and rescue her from her pesky environment of so many sisters and brothers. She is still waiting. This could turn into her life's work.

She says she is willing to wait until he comes along — her Prince Charming. She says she certainly doesn't want to go through life having to pick up dirty clothes. I tell her she should practice just in case. I tell her Prince Charmings just don't come along at the drop of her laundry. I tell her they are mighty hard to find. I certainly had to wait for mine a long time. But she says her dreams will come true. She seems to be willing to work at waiting. It isn't a profitable job but it is relaxing.

I have suggested to one son that he go into law. He has very little difficulty maintaining an argument. He objects to everything. In detail. He presents his case with such persuasion and skill that he nearly convinced me there's nothing wrong with his wearing a gray T-shirt and jeans to a friend's formal wedding. This case however, ended in a hung jury and we used his dad for a judge. The judge ruled in my favor. Our son grumbled "mistrial" and tried to appeal the case. But it didn't work. I told him when he passed the bar exam he could wear anything he wanted at any time. Lawyers can get by with a lot and he said he'd give that serious thought.

I think probably one of our children will bathe for a living. She will just spend her life hopping in and out of the bathtub, rinsing and toweling her hair, using up the world's hot water and soap and leaving a trail of dirty linen wherever she goes. I don't think this is going to be a profitable occupation but no one will ever be able to say she isn't living a clean life. I think that counts for something, don't you?"

Few mothers, I'm sure, would encourage their children to consider witchcraft as an occupation. But, doggone it, one of our daughters shows real talent. I think she was cut out to be a sorceress. For many years, her favorite pastime was pushing a drinking glass around on a Ouija Board and finding out about "life." She spent hours trying to discover if she could borrow her sister's good sweater without getting caught. She said Ouija always steered her right. Ouija gave her permission to drive at the age of 14; attend boy-girl parties before she was ready; stay home from school when she hadn't studied; spray my best cologne on the cat; hit her brother; sleep in an unmade bed and wear a sweatshirt that said "Have One Another." I thought Ouija was a smart-aleck and said so.

I told her if he knew so darn much to ask how I managed to get myself into this particular child-oriented situation. She said Ouija just shuddered and sometimes she heard groans.

I didn't really believe her, but I could certainly understand his attitude.

"LONG LIVE THE QUEEN"

I have friends who like to look in my kitchen cupboards. They are not being nosey but just want to check up to see if it really does take 3,267 dishes per day to feed our family like I told them it did.

Washing, drying and putting dishes away 12 times a day was something I accepted when I signed that good old dotted line on our marriage license, just as my husband had to accept my passion for charge accounts. He complains about that more than I do the dishes.

For many years I have had help in the kitchen. It is called children. It is rotten help. Highly overpaid and underworked.

According to our oldest son, he knew how to flap a dish towel before he learned to shake a rattle. This is not true. I have never taken any child from its crib and plunked it before the kitchen sink.

However, as soon as they discovered how to open the refrigerator door behind my back, they learned to do dishes. Is it my fault some learned earlier than others?

For years our family has engaged in the daily battle of the soap suds. Every meal (bad or good) exploded at the end when kitchen work was assigned. Excuses flew through the house like the dust flies when someone accidentally hits the arm of the sofa.

"I have homework!" (This child NEVER has homework and is flunking math); "I have to wash my hair!" (The hair was washed before school, after school and before dinner.); "I didn't eat ... why should I wash!" (Who consumed one quarter pound of hamburger, two quarts of milk, a mountain of mashed potatoes and half an apple pie ... and he didn't eat?;) "I have a sore on my finger. Dish water hurts!" (Fourteen bandaids are wrapped around one tiny, little gnat bite!)

"It is not my turn!" (This is the same one that flunked math and has worked up a snappy, computer-like system listing all chores and turns for the past three years and the next five.), and "The teacher said I have to watch this television show and it is on right now! (No teacher told anyone to watch Hollywood Squares ... at least I hope they didn't!)

Oh, but wonders of wonders! Something marvelous entered our home recently! It was not a new baby like our youngest wanted or a new dog like our son wanted or an unscratched and undented tiny foreign car like my husband wanted, but an uncomplaining and energetic automatic dishwasher like I wanted.

I genuflect before her when I enter the kitchen. She is the Queen. She is a little noisy when she washes, washes, rinses, rinses, and dries ... but she's quieter than the kids and gets the dishes cleaner.

I love her!

Last week she died. Temporarily I hope. We are waiting for the service man and all her parts. My husband couldn't understand why I wore black and wanted to put her obituary in the paper.

"But I've lost my best friend!" I sobbed. "Where will I hide all the dirty dishes?"

"Put them in the kid's rooms. No one will notice them in

there."

He has a point!

And speaking of kids . . . guess who's back in the kitchen again!

I wish the Queen were well!

MOTHER'S NOSE KNOWS BEST

I am often referred to around our house as "The Nose." This does not trouble me, in fact I am rather complimented. I could be called worse things, you know.

Simply because I have the ability to sniff my way into the hearts — and the clothes hamper — of my family they credit me with mammoth smelling powers.

It is really no big deal. Every mother knows that. Every mother knows that her passages immediately clear the minute the cord is cut. Smelling power comes with the birth certificate.

Before motherhood, my nose was just like everyone elses. Then I became a mother. My nose adjusted quicker than my waistline. Immediately it was alert to lurking odors. It was unusually alert when we were grocery shopping. Mixed in with the fragrance of bananas, beans and beef, I could tell at a sniff when I should abandon the grocery cart and take the baby to the car. My husband continued to shop in innocent non-chalance . . . but not me. And not the other mothers in the store. Throughout the aisles heads came up, nostrils quivered and pained looks crossed their faces. Even those who had left their babies home panicked. A mother's nose is NOT measured in miles.

One or two of our children think my nose is magic. Some way to go down in fame . . . having a magic nose . . . but it has come in handy. I've been able to collar the kid that ate the last chocolate chip cookie with no problem. One whiff of that chocolate breath and it's all over.

"How did you know, Mom?" the child asks, eyes twitching in awesome fear of the mother with the evil nose.

"I can just tell," I answered, giving one big, powerful inhalation just to impress.

Even with a cold I can tell. They think they are home free when I have a stuffed up nose — can get by with anything — even smoking. At least one thought he could. He was 10 and had just tried his first cigar. The smoke wove in and out of his shirt like thread. I could smell him a block away.

He swaggered into the house. I was on the couch munching cough drops.

"Where have you been?" I glared, preparing for the death-blow.

"Playing," he answered smugly.

"You've been smoking. I can smell," I shouted, coming up from the couch in one big leap, my nose trembling.

From that day forward he became a believer — one of my best. He was one of the first to stop putting his underwear under the bed; he no longer kept dead worms in his dresser drawer; he began to bathe without my having to lower him into the tub by force and occasionally he even borrowed his dad's after-shave. I think I warped him.

When he's been gone for very long and comes back home, he pounds his dad on the back, gives his younger sisters a loving tussle, pets the dog . . . and kisses me on the nose.

The nose-sense came in handy when our teen-age daughter started to date. I'm a little older now, and with five daughters the nose soon grows tired and is often sleeping when it should be smelling . . . but I was younger then and my nose was wide-awake.

"He kissed you!" I greeted her at the door. "I can smell the breath-mint."

She became paranoid. She even asked the boys not to call her at home. "My mother's nose can travel over phone wires," she told them. "Anything you say she can smell against you."

But I've noticed that since she's married and has two small children of her own, she, too, has developed the gift. Just the other day when they were here, she exclaimed as she got out of the car, "You're having spice cake for dessert. I could smell it when we turned off the Interstate."

Her husband was surprised. I wasn't.

The one thing that troubles me is the smell I cannot find. Quite often I spend a lot of my spare time trying to track down the scent of a reeking stink. It is sort of like playing Ellery Queen. I seldom fail to meet the challenge . . . and find the smell.

In fact, you'll have to pardon me, I'm going to look for one right now . . . it's beginning to overwhelm . . .

I wonder if it could be this book.

"LONG LIVE THE LITTER BUG"

Ecology is a matter of taste. Our kids are great believers in keeping our skies and streams, highways and national parks free of debris and pollution. In fact they get hysterical if I accidentally let a kleenex fly out of the car window.

"You LITTERED!" they scream. "Did you see that! "SHE littered!"

"I certainly didn't mean to, and I definitely didn't do it on purpose. It was all we could do to keep them from turning me in to the nearest highway patrolman.

And like I said — ecology is just a matter of taste and personally I'm old-fashioned enough to believe that ecology, like charity, begins at home.

No one who is truly interested in anti-pollution would spit sunflower seeds on a shag carpet!

An oil slick in the Pacific is a terrible thing to see, I agree, but so is an empty pizza box in the middle of the living room floor. Especially when it is full of half chewed crusts and we have company coming.

They turn white when they see a popsicle stick on a picnic ground but think nothing of tossing candy wrappers under the couch.

I have gotten to the point where I hardly ever say goodmorning anymore . . . I say "did you pick up your sock?"

Notice I said "sock." Singular! Just plain sock! Our children have two feet each but I end up with only one sock per child.

I buy them all alike at the store but by the time I reach home the socks have developed individual personalities. This means it's thumbs down on the match game. It's impossible to pair a navy blue sock with a turquoise one and get by with it. I know . . . I've tried.

"Quit being sheep," I argue when they yell that no one wears different colored socks to school. I can't even get them to try and set the pace for style. I can almost bet that, if by chance, all the kids suddenly started wearing unmatched socks the darn things would suddenly all look alike.

You'd think that if these smart scientists can get us to the moon they could certainly devote 30 minutes to trying to solve the sock problem.

Someday all of these lost socks are going to show up in the same place at the same time and if ecologists think we are in trouble now . . . just wait until the whole world is buried under a blanket of orlon and wool!

"SORRY, I CAN'T COOK"

I was full of ambition when I was ten. I either wanted to be the right tackle on the Notre Dame football team or the librarian in our small Southern Illinois town. I never wanted to be a cook.

I have always deeply admired those women who can become excited about a cookbook. Things like recipes for hasenpheffer, peach parfait pies and oxtail stew with crescents put them in heaven. Personally, I can't even work up a good sweat... except when I'm trying to make something like hasenpheffer, peach parfait pies or oxtail stew with crescents.

Anyway, I can imagine the reaction if I tried putting oxtail stew (with or without crescents) in front of MY family at mealtime. The children consider themselves gourmets and if it isn't spelled h-a-m-b-u-r-g-e-r they have to be bullied into tasting it. Put a sprig of parsley on something and they immediately suspect Mom's trying to cover up her mistakes again. We have no class to our meals.

I've always envied the soap opera-movie type family that gives us a happy group of little ones eating their gruel and spinach in the kitchen while mother and father loll on a leopard skin rug in front of the fireplace, sipping dry martinis while three-inch steaks broil unattended and out of sight, new and buttery potatoes pop from their pure, brown jackets without the help of human hands and a glorious and crisp salad marinates like magic on the sideboard. Now THAT'S class.

We tried it once. All we got was a lot of static and a rotten martini. Every time I tried sitting down on our tweed davenport to relax the steak began to sizzle and smoke or someone yelled from the kitchen that one of the boys was stealing all the french fries. I knew better, right from the start, not to try and push spinach and gruel off on them.

And each time my husband and I attempted looking Continental, someone wandered out in their pajamas with a milk ring around their mouth. Besides they tasted our meal to death. You know... "can I have a bite... just a little bite?" By the time all seven had bitten there wasn't anything left for us.

We decided that taking our chances at the table with them was better. At least there we have them trained to pass everything to us first and we have an even chance of getting something to eat.

So, we've thrown out any thoughts of grandiose dining and all eat together — among the squashed peas that one child hides beside her plate, gallons of spilled milk and vivid and descriptive conversations that center around biology worm dissections and whose nose bled the most at the wrestling match.

Although I have been lassoed with nervy children I have been twice blessed with a husband who likes to cook. And he is a good cook. When I approach the kitchen the stove heaves a gassy sigh of resignation. When he walks in and gets out the pots and pans even the oven sparkles in anticipation.

He is the sort of cook who can glance at a recipe and create something entirely different and much better than the original. He tosses in this, pitches in that and stirs in two or three drops of something else. If I vary from the recipe by one grain of salt, the whole thing collapses. I really think cooking is a talent... like painting, singing, acting and spelling. You either have it or you don't

Don't misunderstand me. My husband has not adopted the job of cooking for our family as his own. His is the "once-in-awhile, when-the-mood-strikes-him" type of cooking. Mine is the "every-day, three-times-a-day, protect-the-refrigerator-with-my-life-while-I-am-doing-it" type. I think this makes a big difference in attitude, don't you?

Some bright economist, somewhere, came up with the silly statistic that I spend 13.1 hours a week in the kitchen cooking for my family. I spend that much time leaning over my morning coffee trying to wake up. Furthermore, he (and I assume it was a "he" — a bachelor "he") said that, in dollars and cents, I was worth about $32.75. In reality we could peel that down to about $1.25. But for my own personal ego I'd say I'm worth more than $32.75 running around in my stocking feet picking up dirty towels.

I do have to admit that it was a little hard on my husband when he discovered the honeymoon was over and the lady who had taken his name had never done much more than boil an egg or make open-face peanut butter and jelly sandwiches. But he eventually got over the shock, and he evidently found something else about me that pleased him for he keeps mumbling something about "not marrying me for my cooking, anyway."

Oh well, some day, when I'm not so busy in the kitchen, I'll try to figure that one out.

A DANCE AROUND THE MAYPOLE

Now that our children are all growing up we no longer receive crayon-scrawled invitations to school events. I miss them. They used to be the only invitations I ever received.

For years my social life was limited to school plays revolving around "Charlotte's Web," Brownie investitures, PTA open houses, Arbor Day tree plantings and the big event of the year . . . the May Pole dance!

I would tack the creased and wrinkled invitation on the bulletin board . . .

"Please Cum Dance Around Our Maypol"

This was always followed by a more formal and better-spelled summons from the school principal — just in case the original didn't make it home in the lunch box.

"Hello Parents!

It is the first of May . . . and it is the lovely tradition of our school to welcome the Spring Season by dancing around the May Pole and by letting the children share with you the thrill of this exciting experience in rhythm and color."

In other words . . . "Mother! Get up here!"

Now as everyone knows . . . Spring in Nebraska is much like it is anywhere else. It is different than winter. That is — SOMETIMES — it is different than winter. We've gone to bed knowing the meadowlarks were dashing about collecting twigs, lint and aluminum foil for their nests only to wake up the next morning to see them sitting forlorn and frozen on the telephone wires . . . their nests turned to prickly ice cubes overnight.

The first day of May is often a mixture of rain, dust, wind and snow with a 10 a.m. reading of 95 degrees . . . in the shade. I never know from day to day whether to wear a sun bonnet or snow shoes. So I play it safe. I often wear both.

On the day of the May Pole Dance I was gaily dressed in sunglasses and a fur-lined winter parka.

The May Pole was erected on the blacktop beside the school. It wavered and bent in a 55-mile-an-hour wind. Pink rosettes were blowing all over the ground and a hand full of pre-schoolers were fighting for possession of the pink flowers. Dust storms were blurring our vision and the mother's were beginning to look strained . . . hunched up on tiny chairs ripped off from the kindergarten room. My chin rested on my knees and my stomach was cramping.

The May Pole dancers marched out to the tune of the Marine Hymn and took their places. Little hands were chapped from the strong, cold wind and half the girls were crying because they weren't picked to be the May Queen.

The boys, however, (with the exception of the one who WAS picked) were happy because they didn't have to be the May King and wear the corroded crown.

No one would sit by the mothers of the selected King and Queen. They were isolated in a sea of leering faces. I have never

114

been blessed with regal children ... so I leered right along with all the rest.

Then the children began to wind the May Pole. And they wound and they wound and they tangled it all up and two or three of the smaller ones were twisted up in the crepe paper and crying to be released and the music drummed through the whipping wind until the PA system shorted out and all we could hear was the crying and a terrible screech.

This sent the sixth grade boys into spasms of laughter and the Principal into spasms ... period.

Over in the corner of the blacktop the fourth grade teacher was gigging uncontrollably. And she had good reason, because ... during the whole dramatic procedure we had our own drama on the sidelines.

Two little tow-headed twins were going behind all of the scrunched up mothers on the teeny-tiny chairs throwing sand in their hair and down their backs.

The mother of the twins was the only one that I heard comment after it was over ... "It certainly has been a delightful afternoon."

FAMILY FACES SCHOOL'S END

I have never learned to accept the last day of school gracefully. Oh, I know it is coming — like death and dentist bills — but I keep hoping, somehow, someone will forget and the school year will just go on ... and on ... and on.

I keep hoping the school will find our children ... and yours ... so fascinating and delightful and challenging that I will get a nice note home that reads:

Dear Mother:

We have had such great fun this past year we have decided to keep the children in school all summer. Love.

The Teacher

There has been an aching nervousness among my friends and neighbors lately. They are doing a lot of shopping, bridge playing and planning of elaborate morning coffees. Some of the more affluent are mentioning summer camps, supervised teen tours, and patient grandparents. The only ones smug and content are the teachers.

Our children look upon the last day of school in a different way. When it comes their attitudes vary. For instance:

The Kindergartener: The kindergartener is the least affected. They have only gone half-days anyway. They have had no homework. They have learned plenty of new games and their teacher is usually young, pretty and clever. This summer will seem like a very long weekend. They come home on the final day of school much as they do any day "Mommy, I'm home! Can I have a cookie?"

The Third Grader: The third grader is ordinarily very pro-motion conscious. The first words, as the child runs through the door, are: "I got promoted! I got promoted! Wow! Was I scared." Now, this child knows promotion is a cinch. Knows there have been no problems, that the parent-teacher confer-ences have been an exchange of pleasantries. But they are dramatic at this age and the statement is accompanied by a tragic fling of the hand to the forehead and a painful facial grimace. They sink to the couch in exhausted bliss.

The Fifth Grader: The fifth grader is also promotion con-scious. And well they should be. There is good reason. When fifth grader enters the house and shouts "I got promoted! I got promoted! Wow! Was I scared." Mother sinks to the couch in exhausted bliss. Mother was just as scared as fifth grader. While classmates were absorbing interesting and useful things such as adding fractions, the makeup of the celestial sphere and the methods of drawing a neat map, fifth grader was learning how to run the 220, how to construct a faultless spit-ball, developing 72 ways to bug the teacher and majoring in lunch.

The Seventh Grader: The seventh grader enters the house quietly . . . tosses books, gym bag, musical instrument, three science projects (costing $15 apiece and molding), 22 pencil stubs, four sweaters (two of which you have never seen before) and 30 library passes in the corner. Finished with the whole business. It is final. It is over. They will never touch this stuff again and unless removed by mother it could remain in the corner throughout the entire summer — ignored and gathering odors. Stretching lengthening legs in shortening jeans, seventh grader proclaims: "Mom, I'm home! Can I have a cookie?" It is not so far from kindergarten to junior high after all.

The Senior Higher: The senior higher slides in the door, plunks down three tons of notebooks and textbooks, looks the world square in the eye and says "Thank God!" It is time for few words, the direct approach and a lot of action. They leave in the car. Forever.

As for me — I see a summer stretching before me like a giant rubber band . . . just ready to snap! Each morning throughout June, July and August I will probably get up and think to myself . . . "Is this the day for the big snap?" But I will make it.

Mothers are tough.

For there is no doubt September will come again. And then I will be smug and content. And my teacher friends will nervously be doing a lot of shopping, bridge playing and planning whatever elaborate a teacher does ... for in the distance, like death and dentist bills, those school bells will ring again and the door will slam. Only this time the children will be going OUT and I will hear, like the strains of a beautiful waltz ...

"Bye, Mom! See you after school!"

This is the only thing that will get me through the summer.

SINGING SPOUSE'S PRAISES

I know our children expect me to write something about our 25th anniversary.

I know they expect me to write something filled with roses, candlelight, champagne and romantic music.

Instead I can tell you more about radishes, mentholated salve, skinned knees and ring around the collar.

For those of you who are not aware, let me tell you ... 25 years of marriage is NOT all romance. But there is enough sprinkled in between to keep it interesting ... and very nice.

Our honeymoon, for example, was not spectacular. I don't think anyone's honeymoon is. I'm sure I would enjoy it more now than I did 25 years ago — but no one has invited me on one lately. Oh, well.

We went fishing on our honeymoon. It was very hard for me to feel flirtatious when the groom smelled like catfish bait.

To be fair to my husband, I have to admit that I had led him on to believe that I was the husky type of lady that enjoyed being in the fresh air and the out-of-doors. And truthfully when I was with him I didn't particularly look for wolves or boa constrictors as we strolled through the woods on a Sunday afternoon. So, I wasn't really falsifying. I hope you can see that.

But it was with something a little less than pure joy that I sat on the bank, covered with sandburrs, while he fished for white bass, walleyes and catfish with a reverence that almost bordered on heathen worship. However, I pulled up the corners of my mouth by hand, swallowed my fears, bathed three times a day in calomine lotion and cologne and tried hard to be a good sport.

I don't think I fooled him. I never have — not in 25 years. He can read me like a book. And I'm not a best seller. Take my

117

word for it.

As for my husband . . . he "reads" pretty smooth. I can't think of anyone I would rather have for a roommate. Of course, we have to be honest. Robert Redford hasn't asked me . . . and we'll just have to face that possibility if and when it rolls around.

I really and truly think I got the best of the bargain. Let me tell you why.

He has been the type of husband:

— Who manned the mop bucket and still said "I Love You" after a bout of morning sickness . . .

— Who doesn't really seem to mind because I can't cook . . .

— Who doesn't care (and neither do I) that both our wedding bands are wearing out a little at the edges — and so are we.

— Who obviously doesn't let it bother him that I talk 20 times more than he does . . .

— Who sometimes listens to me . . .

He's the kind of husband who looks at me in the morning when my hair and eyes are matted, my cheekbones are dragging and my facial features puckered and doesn't scream . . . and still invites me for a weekend at a motel — now and then.

— Who sometimes buys me pots and pans for my birthday, a vacuum cleaner for Christmas and a sheer nightie for Valentine's Day . . .

— Who sent a lovely bouquet of flowers to my office the day after I lost the first of many arguments with our oldest son with a message that said . . . "Have a Happy Day" . . .

— Who changed the course of my life the first time he said "hello."

— Who takes out the garbage without being asked.

— Who will probably never make a million dollars but has an ever-ending bank account of tenderness to draw on whenever I need it . . . and I write a lot of checks, believe me . . .

— Who makes it very plain and in very strong language that he will not share bed and board with all the furry little animals that I want to adopt and who insists they remain outside his home where they belong and who shuts his eyes and pretends not to notice when I sneak them in the back door . . .

— Who accepts my shabby housecoat without nausea . . .

— Who doesn't take it personally and pout when I move to the couch because he snores . . .

— Who doesn't fly into a rage (just a slight tremor) at the purchase of a new dress . . .

— Who is a pussycat when it comes to his children . . .

— And a tiger when it comes to his wife . . .

— He's the kind of husband that seems to have a terminal case of love . . .

I hope he never recovers!

WEAR AND TEAR ON MOTHER

School has started again — I will pause here for silent prayer — I am in the recovery room stage from "shopping for school clothing."

I think it will be Christmas before I fully recover. By then they will have outgrown and outworn everything and it will be time to start over again. I may start drinking.

When our children were eight or nine I didn't think it was so bad. I did what I thought was necessary with little interference. I saw to it each one had at least one sweatshirt, complete with name on it, and a neat pencil box. The sturdy corduroys plaid shirts, jumpers and petticoats fell right into line and were accepted without much fuss.

Anyone older than that has become messy . . . progressively so upon reaching junior and senior high age.

I would rather go to the dentist than go school shopping with our children. Don't get me wrong — some of our best friends are dentists — but I am not a lover of air-filled drills and cold-water squirters, nor am I a lover of going into a shop with teenagers.

First of all, they are sullen because I am with them at all. They much prefer spending my money with their best friends. I tried the "independent choice" approach once and let them shop alone. One of our daughters ended up with a pair of $40 shoes, a varied-colored animal fur jacket and three pair of underpants as her complete back-to-school wardrobe. It was a long year — for her and for me.

And they seem to resent an honest opinion. Let me say how nice they look, how well something fits and how the color becomes them and the sale is lost. They become immediately suspicious of anything I approve of.

"No one wears anything like this," they said, tossing long hair and stomping back into the fitting room. Never mind that we have just watched three homecoming candidates from their school walk by wearing identical outfits to the one just rejected.

The mothers of the candidates were smart. They muttered "Gross" the minute they saw their daughters' clothing.

I'm the one who pushes for new clothes for school. It's a fetish with me. I think our children should start out fresh in September with something besides cutoffs and mud-coated tennis shoes. Call me old-fashioned. My husband thinks they should

119

wear what they like as long as it costs under $10.

When we do get to the store one runs off to the pet department, one to records, and one hangs around cosmetics. It takes me 30 minutes of our alloted 90 minutes of shopping time to round them all up. We spend another 30 minutes arguing about wearing halter tops to school and 15 fighting over shoes.

I just can't bear to send our children to school without a pair of new shoes. We've always bought new school shoes and I suppose we always will. The fact that the children don't wear them has not altered this. No one sees them anyway because pants legs cover them up.

It has been hard for me to adjust to seeing our daughters wear clothes that fit their two older brothers perfectly. One of the boys is six feet tall, the other almost there. The girls measure about 5-3.

When I guide them to the counter where they have nice double-knit slacks, with matching, long-sleeved, practical blouses, they roll their eyes, punch each other, make funny noises, insult the fashion buyer's choice and generally cause a major disturbance. That's when I toss my head and stomp off to the housewares department shouting, "Wear what you like . . . see if I care." Or I visit with other glazed-over mothers who are standing around with their arms full of clothes no one wants.

Once in awhile — just once in awhile — our children fool me.

For instance, the last time we went shopping our senior high student came out to model the outfit she had chosen.

She looked so nice. The skirt fit smoothly and gracefully. It was a nice color and the newest fashion length. She had chosen a soft, feminine blouse that complimented her figure. A small delicate turquoise necklace was around her neck. Her shoes were the type to walk in and not to fell a forest. She had put on a pair of pantyhose. A gasp went up among the mothers circling the fitting room area. They all turned to see what I would say as our daughter gracefully turned in front of me.

"Gross!" I said.

Guess what she wore the first day of school!

BEING A COMFORTABLE 40

I have a friend who celebrated her 40th birthday this past week. I have not seen her to wish her a happy birthday. And she will not answer her telephone. Her husband told me all she does is sit in front of the mirror and cry.

I don't think she should do that — not at all. She shouldn't let it bother her so much. Being 40 is not so bad. It's not so good, but it's not so bad. After all, it is not the end of the world. It doesn't necessarily mean she is over the hill. It just means she is on the edge and that she has to hang on a little tighter and try a little harder to keep from being dumped over.

Having passed this rocky part of my life a few years ago, and recovering nicely thank you, I would like to pass on a few suggestions for her that could smooth the road a little.

(1) Never admit to anyone that you ARE 40. Your mother knows, of course, but she won't squeal for personal reasons; your best friends know but they aren't going to tell because they don't want to be associated with a has-been and after the first day or so your husband won't remember and you might be able to fool him forever. Besides, he is probably worried because he is 50 and has his own problems now. The only ones you want to watch out for are your children. They view anyone over 40 as being grizzled and brittle-boned. As far as they are concerned, you have definitely lost your usefulness. You are no longer effective anywhere . . . They will be quick to spread the news. One might even put it in the school paper. It's a cinch they will use it as a topic in Current Events class.

(2) Leave all cosmetics, with the exception of lipstick and blush, out of sight. This annoys guests who snoop in your bathroom for things like hormone creams, body lotions, and wrinkle removers. Place, in an obvious corner of your vanity, a teenage acne medicine with your name on the bottle.

(3) Buy a clothes line and hang out sheets early in the morning two or three times a week. Older neighbors will be convinced that only the very young have enough energy to hang clothes. Throw in a diaper or two. This will confuse them and add to your image.

(4) NEVER, NEVER complain about arthritis, bursitis, thin blood, vitamin deficiencies or a bad back . . . or about being too warm. Especially avoid talking about being too warm. That's a dead giveaway, if you ask me.

(5) You are allowed a migraine once in awhile. But you must casually mention side effects of "the pill" when you pass your hand over your forehead. This will raise some eyebrows and deflect the conversation from your age. I suppose, if you want, you can have a fainting spell just as long as it is done gracefully. Once a year close all the drapes, send the children to friends, turn off your phone, and have a complete and solid nervous breakdown all by yourself. This helps tremendously.

(6) Show enthusiasm for such things as children's birthday parties, parent-teacher conferences, committee memberships and attending morning coffees. Under no circumstances should you ever admit that these things might possibly bore

121

you stiff. Be the first to volunteer for any organizational job. Often a woman's age is measured by how fast she says "I'll do it." The older they are the longer they take to volunteer for anything.

(7) Have lots of babies. Theoretically, this is supposed to keep you young. However, I'd watch this particular rule carefully. Too many babies and it really won't matter how old you are. You won't care.

(8) Take plenty of long, fast walks. This will keep you in shape for things to come. If you pick rainy days people will really be impressed. It might kill you off but just think how young you will look when you go.

(9) Wear your high school class ring, discreetly turned to hide the date, and once in awhile put on your cheerleader's outfit and go outside in the front yard and turn cartwheels. Be sure and invite me over to watch!

(10) Do not admit that the checkout boy at the grocery store looks like he is 10 years old and too young to work or that the graduating class from Senior High all look like eighth graders. Hire only baby sitters in their early 60s when your husband is scheduled to drive them home. Maybe you'd better make it early 70s . . . after all he is 50 and you know how strange they get.

I hope you had a happy birthday.

Who knows . . . it may be your last!

FEMALE ATHLETES BLOSSOM

I thought I was home free when both of our sons graduated from high school and were no longer involved in competitive sports.

No more gym bags full of UFO's (unidentifiable foul objects); no more late night dinners waiting for practice to be over; no more long hours spent on the bleachers hoping to see our son go in to play; no more rotten thoughts about the coach because our son did not go in to play; no more fears of broken bones, torn ligaments and busted heads.

We only had girls left at home and ordinarily girls are considered safe at least concerning athletics. Athletes, however, are a different story. Girls do like athletes and sometimes attend the games, not to watch the skill and deftness of the players . . . but to flirt. This does not require practice or coaching. It is built-in.

Suddenly the government and the school system discovered we had three girls tucked securely away at home . . . eating meals on time, laundering clothes that didn't make me gag, loose, released and joyous.

"She's getting far too complacent," they conspired. "Her wrinkles are even beginning to look relaxed. We can't have that. We certainly can't."

So they initiated girls' sports.

And because our children cannot bear to see a light on in the school building without being there, our daughters, too, became a part of the sports program.

My husband said it was my fault. "What can you expect," he argued, "when they have a mother who claims her utmost ambition at the age of 16 was playing right tackle on the football team?"

I didn't mind his bringing up my past ambitions. I really didn't. But what hurt was the fact he felt I might have made first-string if they would have let me play. I realize I am blessed with a mature figure — but right tackle! Oh well.

This time things were different. The gym bags still had the usual gamy scent as they marched across the utility room floor (sometimes on their own power) but now the waft of cologne and mascara intermingled with other curious odors. It was a little better. Not much . . . but a little. And I had more than an even chance of recognizing the contents. With the boys, I was wrought with constant mystery.

We still had to worry about busted heads and broken bones and occasionally we had sensational thoughts about the coaches but the one plus we found in having girls involved in sports wiped out most of the minuses.

OUR DAUGHTERS RECOGNIZED US AS THEIR PARENTS.

For years, any son of ours involved in any sporting event was immediately an orphan — by choice. He did not speak or wave in recognition as we sat cheering on the sidelines. We became known as the invisible Mom and Dad.

When he passed before us as we sat on the bleachers his chin automatically fell to his chest in reflex. The only way I knew it was him was the uniform number. Team members whose parents were not there took to the field in long, strong strides while our son stumbled, unseeing, around the sidelines, head planted between his knees, living in fear his mother would stand up and wave. I never did. I knew better. I was warned.

"Don't come near me," he said, terror in his eyes, the first time he played in public. "Not even if I'm crushed and dying. Don't come near me." And I didn't.

The girls, on the other hand, are glad we are there. They wave first. With both hands. And they talk to us. In sign language, with exaggerated facial features and funny gestures. Some-times I'm stunned. Their conversations are not selective.

"Did I get any mail?" they signal. "Can I sleep over? There's a dance Friday night. Can I go? I got an A in Government! One of the teachers is pregnant. She isn't married! How does my hair look? Does my uniform bag? Where are my red socks? I want a jumpsuit! Why are you wearing Daddy's sweater?" etc. etc. etc.

I am an emotional wreck before the whistle blows ending the game. You see, I can understand her perfectly — and I'm sure most of the spectators can. I knew this for sure when our team made the winning point and none of the home crowd clapped. That was during the pregnant teacher conversation. The air in the auditorium was chilled in silence. I sort of wanted to put my chin between my knees and become invisible . . . like the Good Old Days.

But I didn't. And I won't. It is fun to watch girls play. They seldom stop talking, poking each other and giggling. They pause only long enough to jump up and scream in triumph or sit down and moan in defeat. They are as active on the bench as they are off it and playing. It is a happy occasion, win or lose.

And who cheers them on and is their biggest and loudest fan? You guessed it. That old-time dreamer . . . the mythical and imaginary right tackle on the football team.

Sometimes I wish I were young again.

"HOW DO YOU DO SPRING"

How do you do, Spring! Thank you for coming. Are you plan-ning to stay around now . . . for good? I certainly hope so. Lately it seems you have been changing your weather-mind about as often as our teen-agers change their clothes before they go to school in the morning. And that's a lot. But then you don't pile everything up in one corner or in the middle of the world like they do their clothes. At least you let the wind blow things about. I can say that in your favor.

Oh, I'm not complaining, Spring. Goodness knows I'm used to living with children whose body temps run hot and cold like a water faucet. Your temperature tantrums don't bother me a bit.

It seems funny to me, though, that one of our sons can zip right out to get the mail, barefoot, shirtless and hatless, when HE is expecting a letter without so much as a "Brrrrrr," but let me ask him to get meat from the deep freeze in the basement and he fears frost bite. I tell him "Put on mittens!" and I get the old "mother is trying to be clever again" groan.

I groan occasionally too. I groan as I watch our 14-year-old break out in chapped skin right before my eyes when I inform her she may not have, in April, a full-length, fur-trimmed, maxi-coat that costs about as much as a new car.

"But I freeze, mother, I truly freeze!" And she looks so cold standing there in the department store with nothing but a frayed army jacket on. Sympathetic tears jump into my eyes. I weaken. I pledge to go without the new lipstick I had promised myself (after all I can always bite my lips for color) and bought the coat. I felt instantly warm on the inside because now she would be warm on the outside. So summer is only a few weeks ... or days ... ahead. So what? I went to bed with "good mother" thoughts instead of the usual "I've sure been a witch today" attitude. Funny, but I slept better too.

The next morning I saw her in the front yard playing with the cat. I could barely see her through the foggy, snowy haze. She was gliding over the ice, clad in a T-shirt and short shorts. Her light blue arms and legs went well with the red and white striped shirt.

I immediately slipped back into my witch's robes. "Well, nobody wears a coat!" she gasped, unbelievably, when I ask her where was the new coat we had just bought. The dining room chair was wearing the new coat. The chair wears the coat more than she does. I'm wondering if rubbing fur briskly against the mouth would bring color. Maybe then, the coat would be useful and I'd have some sort of lipstick. I can always try it.

Even when they do wear a coat . . . they do not button it. "Button your coat!" I hiss, between blasts of cold air, as we walk down the street together. I have to hiss loud for after the age of three the children will not voluntarily walk next to their mother in public. There is a lot of hissing space between us.

That is, until we meet our family doctor. The family doctor who has always had grave doubts about my ability to care properly for so many children. But then he delivered them all . . . I think he is partially responsible . . . don't you?

When we meet our family doctor the child, who has until now been skipping merrily ahead of me like a sunflower on a hot July afternoon, adheres to my side like scotch tape. He suddenly starts to shiver and shake and with chattering teeth greets his friend, the family doctor with a wistful and woebegone look of total neglect. Little hands flutter to a bared chest as if to say "I'd button my coat up . . . but SHE won't let me!" I resolve the next time I take anyone to town I am going to sew them into their coats. With wire! Or rivets!

Quite often Spring, I feel like taking the advice of some of my wiser friends and offer a little more prayer at my house and a little less peanut butter.

"GOOD MOTHERS AREN'T HARD TO FIND — THEY ARE JUST HIDING."

It isn't hard to be a good mother. All you need is a strong back, a flexible heart, 26 hands and a packet of gold safety pins. These are necessary. Unnecessary, but nice, are your very own potato peeler, eyebrow tweezers and stationery. If you have all of these (and know where they are at all times) you could consider yourself "Queen of the Block."

Unfortunately, my potato peeler is usually in the garbage; I buy three tweezers a week and my eyebrows still look like I am perpetually frightened, and the stationery I ordinarily end up using has little red and white polka-dotted elfs sitting under bright yellow toadstools.

But I have a strong back. I find a strong back useful when I have to move a card table fort, draped with 14 blankets, from the living room before the minister arrives; to rearrange the bedroom furniture before my husband comes home so that the worn spot in the carpet will show and my argument for a new one will be solidified; to move the bedroom furniture back where it was in the first place when the argument doesn't work; to carry the dog outside when he won't go out any other way; to carry the third grader out to the school bus when HE won't go any other way; to whip the garbage out to the collection point (my flexible heart comes in handy here when I have to stumble over a 17-year-old son's legs in order to whip the garbage out to the collection point); to bend over the garbage to search for my lost potato peeler and to haul packages around during dollar days. Of course hauling packages in no way compares to hauling card tables, furniture, children, dogs or garbage. Packages are a labor of love.

The flexible heart is nice during parent-teacher conferences when you don't know for sure whose side to be on; or when only three members of the family show up for dinner after having planned a marvelous, five course meal (from scratch . . . no boxes); or when ALL members of the family show up (complete with guests) when you have baloney sandwiches and curdled tomato soup; or when your precious kindergartner falls in love with his teacher and before that he loved you best; or when your precious husband falls in love with golf and before that he loved you best and when the television doesn't work during Sesame Street.

I use my 26 hands to pet children, pet cats, prepare food, sew on buttons, mend a stuffed animal, iron a blouse, wipe up spills, answer the phone, sort socks, find a lost math paper, read the birth column in the paper, water a plant, kill a fly, adjust a runaway dishwasher, rinse a pair of hose, scrape mud from a shoe, staple a term paper, comb a ponytail, polish nose spots from the window, wind up paper towels, change a light bulb, adjust the stove, unstick "happy stickers" from the kitchen cabinets, find a salt shaker, fill a salt shaker and take aspirin . . . all in 30 minutes.

And as far as I'm concerned, only a mother who is on the next level and a step away from angelhood can exist without safety pins . . . gold preferred. I think every expectant mother should be presented a packet of pins as she is wheeled into the labor room. In the long-run they will prove to be more important than the American Beauty roses her husband sends; or the cute cards her friends send; or the volumes of advice the new grandmother sends. A packet of safety pins might well save her life . . . and her sanity at three o'clock in the morning.

They can be used during those sleepy, early morning hours to poke holes in stuck nipples, to poke holes in stubborn nose drop bottles and to poke holes in sleeping fathers.

Safety pins are good to close kimonas, diapers, sweaters, little bonnets, buntings and the underarm seam on Mother's dress on Sunday morning . . . on the way to church. They are great to unstick the cracks in the kitchen table; to temporarily pin the ruffling around the Early American chair 10 minutes before company comes; to hitch up a toddler's jeans; to make a Cub Scout presentable (with all badges) before an important Pack meeting and to make a Den Mother presentable before an important Pack meeting.

Yes, I could hardly exist without safety pins. Now, if I could only find that packet I just bought, I'd have it made . . . motherwise. You don't suppose they are in the garbage with this week's potato peeler do you?

"ONLY CHILDREN HAVE MORE FUN"

Occasionally I have the sneaky suspicion that each of our children dreams that he was born to be an only child.

An only child that can watch "Little House On the Prairie" without having to strain his ears and sift the sounds over an older brother's groans and simpering remarks . . . an only child that NEVER has to share the prize in the cereal or the bathroom or a bedroom or wear hand-me-down boots or someone elses outgrown mittens with the dog chews in them . . . an only child that can have an overnight guest without holding a family council to see who else invited an overnight guest . . . an only child who can work a jigsaw puzzle, all alone, without 15

128

other people putting in pieces . . . an only child that can have dad's undivided attention at the dinner table . . .

But, alas, if they were only children they would not have anyone to fight with. Now, that is a dream-popper. Having built-in brawling partners more than makes up for being born in a crowd.

Their wars are not global wars or atomic wars or sabre-rattling wars or hydrogen wars or germ wars (well, I'm not too sure about that — sometimes their rooms look pretty germy to me) or wars that the government will raise taxes and draft people for . . . their wars are picky wars . . . you know, pick, pick, pick!!!

"Look, just look, at the way her elbow bends! Mother, make her quit bending her elbow!"

"I can't stand his eyes! Mother, make him shut his eyes when he is around me!"

"She holds her knees funny. Mother, make her quit using her knees when I am in the room!"

"He sniffles when he walks by me. Mother, make him close his nose!"

Most of the time mother is confused. How can she pick sides? Of course, I blame it all on the hospital where our children were born. If they had only stashed away the classes on bathing, feeding and caring for infants during the four days I was in the maternity ward and showed films on refereeing . . . in the long run it would have worked out better. It wasn't long before they were all feeding, bathing and caring for themselves . . . but they are still fighting!

They have been since they crossed pacifiers in the playpen. For years, two of our children could not digest their breakfast if they sat in full view of each other at the table. Because neither my husband or I are the type to practice "parent effectiveness" early in the morning and be a jolly, jolly mommy and daddy, we solved this by lining up seven or eight cereal boxes — tall cereal boxes — in the middle of the table, cutting off their view of each other. This was hard on the budget but easy on the nerves. Those who liked each other thought it was great. They had a multiple choice of cereal.

I also thought this was a perfectly good solution to a sticky problem. Perhaps everyone eats with dozens of cereal boxes marching across the table. They don't! I found this out by attending a PTA open house where the first grade displayed hand-colored student originals of "A Typical Family Break-fast."

Each picture had a bright table, complete with smiling mother, father and child, tea cups, flowered cereal bowls . . . the sun pouring through the shiny window on a well-laid table. Every picture but one . . . one picture showed a sour mother and father, and a table that had nothing but a row of square, straight boxes on it . . . no bowls, no cups, no smiles, no sunshine . . . just boxes and a name printed very large and correctly spelled . . . LUETH!!

Oh well, I could take that. I just didn't go back to PTA anymore that year. But I couldn't take sleeping with the dog.

But I had to . . . there was no way out. One child was holding the front half of his body and one was holding the back half . . . each trying to take him into their room to spend the night. The dog was yikking and yipping and . . . stretching . . . as no dog should yike and yip and stretch. I was desperate. I was trying to decide how I was going to explain this l-o-o-o-ng dog to my veterinarian.

"All right," I shouted! "If you do not quit this fighting . . . I will sleep with the dog." So there!

They did not quit fighting and the dog did not quit stretching and a mother never lies. I slept with the dog! My husband slept on the couch and said there had never better be anymore silly fights like that!

There are days when I think I am going to do just what a friend of mine said she was . . . divorce the kids and keep my husband.

"DARK JOURNEY"

Recently I hit a major turning point in my life. I drove to another town . . . by myself . . . in the dark.

Perhaps, this does not sound like very much to you. Perhaps, you are the type that can leap in a car, throw it in reverse and back out of the drive, smiling confidently to yourself as you maneuver the steering wheel, temperature control and radio all at the same time. Your mind is free and clear. Your hands are sure and true.

Not me. For me, a trip down the block can be a dark journey. My mind is cluttered . . . crunches filter through my head. But I had to go. I had to attend an important meeting. It was imperative I be there. I have no friends that will ride with me. I asked my husband if he wanted to go. He had a choice . . . drive along with me, insure the safety of his car . . . and his wife, attend an all-ladies meeting OR watch Monday night football. It took about 3½ seconds to make up his mind.

"Be careful," he said. Before the kickoff he walked to the car with me. "You are going very, very early," he observed. The sun is still shining.

"I want to allow plenty of time," I answered.

"Be careful," he said again, a little paler this time. His hands trembled as he stroked the left rear bumper. It had just been repaired. It cost about $400. He was starting to weigh the value of watching the Vikings against the value of the rear end of his car. I could tell.

"Don't drive too fast," he sighed, giving in to his baser needs. Now that was really unnecessary. He knows I don't drive too fast. Of all things . . . that's one thing I won't do. He knows I'm the one that tightens my lips, shoves my feet into the floorboard and watches for police when HE'S driving. He knows that. We discuss it often enough.

I made it out of the driveway fine. I was very hot. I stopped the car to turn on the air-conditioning. It had to be adjusted. It took awhile, I have to admit, but I don't know why that man behind me had to honk so loud or so long. If he wanted to get somewhere that fast, "Call an ambulance," I always say. Silly goose.

Threading my way down to and on to the main highway was easy. The man with the honking horn had finally turned off on a side street. He didn't use his turn signals or anything. He just sort of whipped and twisted his car around at the last minute. I don't think that particular street was on his original route.

I was glad he was gone. He was bothering me. He was driving so close behind me that every time I looked into the rear view mirror all I could see was his teeth. And I could read his lips. Oh, my!

Barreling down the road at 30 miles per hour, I felt pretty smooth. I wasn't doing so bad. I began to think I might even make it. Perhaps I could take a trip to Denver sometime, or San Francisco . . . or maybe even New York. Or — who knows — The Indianapolis "500."

The car approaching me blinked his lights. "Fresh," I thought. Then I noticed it was dark outside. Very dark. I could hardly see. I was driving without lights.

I put on the headlights. The windshield wipers snapped on. I had certainly failed somewhere. Another driver blinked his lights. "Oh shut up!" I screamed, trying to drown out the scrape of the wipers as they did a buck and wing across the window. It was still very dark. I pushed another button. The cigarette lighter popped out. I am growing very tired of pulling and pushing knobs. I finally find the right one. The lights were very, very bright and cars were still blinking but I didn't care. I was almost there, and I was still alive.

The return trip was not half-bad. I had had a good rest. I had slept through the meeting. I tried to hurry home. I drove 35 m.p.h. I just knew my husband had been spending his evening pacing the floor, wringing his hands, visualizing pictures of my twisted body and his car's twisted rear-end beside the road.

He was sound asleep in his chair when I burst through the door triumphantly, rattling the car keys. Why, he didn't even know I was home.

And when you get right down to it . . . I don't think he cared!

CB RADIO LANGUAGE BAFFLING

We have something new. No, Virginia it is not a brand new dining room set, or a couch for the living room . . . not even new curtains at the windows. It is something far more practical and useful, my husband claims.

It is a CB radio — in our car. I cannot get used to it. It is very hard for me to operate.

I have always been a citizen of this country and spoken its language. And I've gotten along pretty well, up until now. If there is one thing I have had confidence in . . . it is my ability to talk. I am usually able to carry on a coherent conversation. But I have lost that confidence since I tried talking on our CB.

It is all my husband's fault. He bought it, installed it and he's the one who urged me to talk on it. "Go ahead," he said. "It's fun. Why, with the way you like to talk . . . you should be a natural." I soon proved him wrong.

I knew the first word was "Breaker." That's how you get everyone's attention. I knew that. And I got it out beautifully. I sounded professional . . . almost.

A voice boomed back at me, "Yeah, there, Breaker. Got 'shure ears on?"

I grabbed my head. They were still there. I was glad.

"Bear up ahead," the voice informed calmly.

"Oh my God!" I shouted. I'm terribly afraid of bears.

"He just did a flip-flop. Watch it. He's headed down."

"The poor thing," I replied. I don't like bears and an injured one, flip-flopping around out there . . . couldn't that be dangerous?

"Why don't you do something?" I shouted. I was getting upset.

So was my husband. His face was turning yellow. The wires on the radio crackled . . . our reception was fading. Maybe I had broken our CB.

Suddenly the voice came back. "Have you got a copy?"

"I'm sorry," I answered quickly, and with some pride. "I sent that in a few days ago. My deadline is Monday noon." My goodness, I thought, someone out there reads my column and talks about it on the CB and everything. "Isn't that nice?" I asked my husband.

"He doesn't mean your column, silly," clinching his teeth and the steering wheel. "He means "where are you located?"

"What's your mile marker?" the voice asked.

He sounded weary.

"Good heavens, I don't know. I can't see those little things without my glasses. Besides we're driving too fast."

"Don't say that!" my husband hissed. "Don't ever say that. You don't know who is listening. Bears might be listening."

"That's cute," I laughed softly.

"I think I'll go now," the voice broke in.

He didn't sound so much like C. W. McCall any more.

A strange voice came over the radio. "Breaker one-nine. For someone. Not the lady, please."

"Go Break!" Old C. W. was back. He sounded better.

"Hey there, good buddy," the stranger said. "I need some Texas road conditions. Ten-four."

"Sorry, good buddy," C. W.'s voice sounded stronger and stronger. They must be real close friends, I thought.

The stranger snorted a little. "Last time I was down that way it was so dry I saw the trees fighting over a dog."

I thought that was funny. I laughed.

Accidentally I pushed the microphone button down. Evidently I laughed very loud.

C. W. yelled out in pain. I must have hurt him or something. His language was terrible.

"I don't think he should say things like that," I exclaimed.

"Somehow I feel the FCC will forgive him this time," my husband said, his nostrils flaring.

"Come back, good buddy," C. W. had returned. "I got walked on."

"Oh dear, I bet that hurt," I said into the microphone. "Is there anything I can do? I've had first aid in Girl Scouts."

C. W. groaned. He seemed to be wearing out. "I'm down on the side," he announced.

"That poor man," I said as I turned to my husband. "I think he just had an accident. Shouldn't we stop and help him or something?"

My husband didn't answer. He reached across the car and took the microphone from my hand. In doing so, he nearly ran off the road. It was a close call.

Well, I tell you what I think. With all those bears and the flip-flopping and getting walked on and falling down on the side . . . personally, I think CBs are dangerous, and I'd rather

have new curtains.
At least they don't talk back.

AN UPSTAIRS ADVENTURE

Our house has an upstairs. We keep the children up there.

Unless forced I do not enter this part of the house. I blame this on a bad back and the inability to climb stairs gracefully. In reality I can't stand the mess.

True, sometimes the downstairs becomes a little jammed with yesterday's newspapers, mail-order catalogs, sewing thread, thimbles, pantyhose, peanuts and pear skins . . . but, after all, these are all things I need or might need at the tip of my fingers, in order to conduct the everyday business of being a contented homemaker. These things are the tools of my trade.

These things are also things that can be stashed in an available drawer the minute unannounced company drives up outside. In a businesslike and systematic manner I have designated a few cabinet drawers for just such emergencies. You should try it. As long as I don't forget them. When I do that I don't think I'm quite so smart.

But the upstairs! There just aren't enough cabinet drawers in the world to hold the overflow. It is permeated with wet tennis shoes and damp sweatshirts. Here lies a record player, a guitar, a dead Beatle poster, a hair dryer, an antique stereo, three or four poor plants gasping for oxygen, assorted Barbie boots, pompoms and sunflower seeds.

In there, somewhere are beds and closets.

In trying to shame the children into some sort of reasonable tidiness, I say with genuine concern, "What will your friends think of this mess when they come over?"

"Oh, that's O.K., Mom," one answers. "Their rooms are messier than this."

Now, I don't believe this — not for a minute — but it certainly helps my morale to think that perhaps some other mother . . . somewhere . . . lives under the same conditions as I do.

I am content for awhile and let up on the cleaning routine.

However, the day finally comes when I can stand it no longer . . . when the dog (and Dad) balk at going upstairs. Then I know it is time. The limit has been reached.

The word "CLEAN" travels through the house like the hiss of a snake. Everyone disappears. Even the dog. (And Dad.)

But I'm on to that old trick. Can't fool me. I just stand in the middle of the dining room and yell, "It's time to eat! We're having hamburgers!"

Everyone reappears like magic. It always works. I think it always will.

Yet, just as soon as they find out I am not going to feed them hamburgers (at 9:30 a.m.) they start complaining. Always they are complaining.

"But what's dirty about it?" they say to demented mother. "It's a perfectly nice bedroom."

"For Spiders!" demented mother answers sharply and with quick wit, handing them a mop and last year's tee shirts. "Get busy!"

Now, this may seem cruel to those of you who are:
1. Unmarried;
2. Childless;
3. Rich;
4. A grandmother.

But look at it this way — they made the mess — they can darn well clean it up. I will condescend to pick up after toddlers, any visitors who stay overnight and I'm very kind if the children are running a temperature. I feel I do my share.

You know what it is, don't you? It's that silly Mary Poppins with her dumb umbrella and spoonful of sugar that has messed up things for ordinary mothers.

Every child dreams of the day when she will fly down their chimney and make their lives happy and easy, neat and tidy, calm and composed.

I'll clean her boots and water the flower on her hat if she'll stay at our house.

I could certainly use her. Well, couldn't you?

Think about it!

TRYING TO TRAIN LITTLE PATRIOTS

The Fourth of July gives me a chance to push patriotism.

Now, I don't know about your children but ours were not born patriotic. They were born with overactive tear ducts, diaper rash and hooked on pacifiers but nothing in their birth certificates pointed to patriotism. I have had to work on that.

For as many summers as I can remember I arranged museum tours for my family living in eternal hope that the experience would rub off and they would become history buffs.

I had heard of culture-starved children who stood and gaped

by the hour at glassed-in mocassins, reliving our country's fine history.

Ours seemed more interested in:

(1) Carefully studying all boys between the ages of 14 and 20;

(2) Picking up and handling everything marked "Do Not Touch";

(3) Draping themselves around the souvenir counter;

(4) Pushing pennies into the gum ball machines;

(5) Peeking under the skirts of the wax dummies.

I am usually the tour guide. My husband has the ability to sleep through situations he has no control of. And he is walking around.

I answer questions like . . .

"No, I do not think there is a pop machine in the museum."

"No, you cannot buy a perfect bone-structured replica of a buffalo for $19.88. It is made of plastic."

"No, I don't care if daddy did say it was OK. Daddy isn't himself."

"No, the big bird is not alive. It is stuffed."

"No, I do not know what they stuff it with. It is called a vulture. They eat things."

"No, it will not eat you. The big bird is dead. It is stuffed."

"No, it is not stuffed with little sisters like your big brother told you."

"No, Daddy is not asleep. I know he is walking with his eyes shut. He is thinking."

I am happy to report that somewhere-somehow-something did rub off. Our children are patriotic. We celebrate the Fourth of July with a flourish. In fact, one year we had to discourage our oldest son from packing his gym bag and running down to join the marines. He was 12 years old. We promised him he could conduct flag ceremonies in honor of our country's birthday instead.

He hauled us all out of bed on that particular Fourth of July by the dawn's early light. It was drizzling rain and very damp and chilly. It reminded me of Valley Forge.

"Let's all go back to bed where it is warm and dry," my husband said. "We cannot put the flag up in the rain."

Our son, in systematic investigation, had discovered that the modern-day method was to hang the flag out despite the weather. I didn't agree. But I didn't want to say anything and squelch a 12-year-old's patriotism. I didn't think Congress would care. Like my husband, I had been taught that a drop of water on the flag was the first step to treason. Letting it touch the ground was second.

Our son knew this one too. When his little sister, half-asleep and trembling from the cold let her corner sag a bit he shouted,

"DON'T LET THE FLAG TOUCH THE GROUND!!"

Out of pure fright she dropped her whole corner.

I assured her not to mind what her brother said. She would not be put in chains in a dungeon and the President of the United States would not personally come to Nebraska to gag and chain her and put her there. The glare I gave our son could only be matched by the rocket's red. She calmed down and stopped sobbing and we went on with the ceremony.

All nine of us stood at attention as the flag made its jerky trip up the flag pole. Goose bumps appeared on my arms. Some from patriotism and some from chill.

Then our son sprang his surprise. He played reveille on his cornet — as only a 12-year-old who doesn't practice can play reveille on a cornet.

This had a sweeping impact on all neighbors within the immediate block. Dogs barked, cats flew up trees, babies screamed, doors opened and people streaked from their homes with terrorized expressions on their faces. Our son started to swing into "My Country 'Tis Of Thee." My husband prevented this by removing the mouthpiece from the cornet.

Our neighbors with muddy bare feet and damp pajamas went back inside their houses to dress. Like it or not their Foruth of July had started — in a very patriotic way!

GUARANTEEING GIFT SECURITY

I started Christmas shopping last May. I bought a twin-sized sheet on sale. I was so proud of myself. Now I cannot find it. There is, of course, a strong possibility that one of three things has happened to it: (1) It became a rose-cluster ghost for Halloween; (2) Augie-Doggie is now sleeping between fresh sheets; (3) It went to college to get an education.

At any rate, I certainly can't give something I cannot find away for Christmas. And that is why I wait until the last minute to do my shopping. If I shop too early, I lose the presents. Or the kids wear them out before the holidays.

One year I gave our oldest daughter a lovely, blue cardigan sweater with three buttons missing and a thread hanging.

"That's strange," my husband said when he saw her modeling her new Christmas outfit. "That sweater looks used."

"You'd look used too," I agreed, "if you'd been wrapped and rewrapped a dozen times, attended two junior high dances and a hay rack ride."

"You mean you let her wear her Christmas present before Christmas?"

I tried to explain that ordinarily I do not give into children's whims; I tried to explain that I like surprises as much as the next person; I tried to explain what it is like to listen to a 15-year-old whimper because she does not have anything to wear; I tried to explain that I sometimes get headaches; I tried to explain that obviously he has never been a mother. He kept pushing.

"How did she know she was getting that sweater for Christmas?"

Because she looked — that's how. It's as simple as that. Hardly any of our children can stand the suspense of Christmas. They become paranoid. One even runs a temperature.

Each year I spend weeks scheming, blue-printing and planning my "hide-the-presents" strategy. It is carefully contrived and cleverly designed. I call it "Operation Stash."

"There now," I said smugly to myself, as I removed the ceiling tile from the family room and placed the Christmas gifts securely on the rafters. "They will not find them this year." Two days later I saw a ladder in the middle of the room, the ceiling looked screwy and bright ribbons curled from the cracks in the tile. They had me again.

Once we thought we had them outwitted. We took the presents to my dad's house. We hid them in his spare bedroom. He looked but that was OK. This worked very well as far as keeping the children in suspense. It worked too well. We were all in suspense. We had forgotten what we bought. After one of the boys ended up with nothing for Christmas but three dump trucks and 18 pair of underpants we dropped that idea . . . and went to the locked door.

This project took the most time, planning and money. My husband designed an expensive, intricate, child-proof lock-and-key system for our bedroom door. We put the presents in there . . . carefully catalogued and listed as to content.

This was a real feeling of security. (In more ways then one . . . I really liked that locked door for lots of reasons). We patted each other on the back and congratulated ourselves for being so devilishly clever. My husband said to me, "This time we have them for sure . . . no one, absolutely no one, can pick that lock." I hid the key under the dishwashing detergent. I was positive they would never look there. I was right. It would have been much too simple for them to find the key and unlock the door.

They became cat burglars.

While other children danced around their fairy Christmas trees, baked sweetmeats and cookies, planned homemade gifts for mommy and daddy, our children studied old films of Bonnie and Clyde. Quietly and methodically they collected tools from the neighbors, assigned jobs and plotted their caper.

139

They pulled it off while my husband and I attended a holiday party. The perfect crime . . . almost.

We returned from the party full of confidence and Christmas Cheer. My husband gleefully unlocked the bedroom door. "Boy," he said, "we sure fooled them this year. No one, absolutely no one could get into this room — not without taking the door off the hinges."

We looked at each other. They wouldn't! They had.

Running into the room I glanced around . . . Barbie had changed her dress. The Hot Wheels were still hot. A candy cane lay, licked, on the floor. An inflated Santa sat on the foot of our bed with a frown on his face. Santa was mad. So was I!

This year I am really going to fool them . . .

I just won't buy any presents . . .

How do you like that!

CHRISTMAS LETTER FANTASIES

Our annual Christmas letter lacks class. I don't think it is all my fault though. I'm certainly not going to lie about our lifestyle just to make our Christmas cards romantic and fanciful. Would you?

My husband said I didn't need to tell everything. He said I didn't need to write about how high the gas bill was or that the dog's spaying came too late or that our neighbors have marital problems. He said that was no one else's business. I told him that was probably the most excitement we had all year. He didn't believe me. He said I provided a lot more than that. I wonder what he meant. I didn't ask.

Our Christmas letter is really colorless — I will say that. How I would love to send one out like this:

"Season's Greetings to our millions of close friends:

Do hope you have had as nice a year as we have!

Lover and I and the children spent a month enjoying our annual fishing spree off the coast of Puerto Rico. A killer shark brushed by our boat as we trolled. The others on the boat were horrified but not Lover. He just raised his hand — said "Stay," in that masterful voice of his and that li'l old shark just melted into the waves. The captain and crew applauded.

Then on June 30 Lover and I flew to London, England, and thus began a very different vacation. We left the dear children with our trustworthy housekeeper.

We spent two days touring castles and looking up ancestors

and on Monday went into London proper, saw the Crown Jewels, went for a ride on the Thames, said a quickie hello to the Queen and boarded the plane for Amsterdam. The flight was faultless. Oh, we had one incident. A hijacker. But Lover just put up his hand, calmly said "Stay," and the hijacker threw down his gun and sobbed to be forgiven. The captain and the crew applauded.

From Amsterdam we rode to Bonn, Germany, where we visited former neighbors, Jan and Stan. They rented a VW bus and we all piled in for a 3½-week tour of the country. I cannot tell you what a wonderful time we had. A boat ride on the Rhine, castle after castle, nuts in the forests, an ancestor or two. Indescribable!

From Bonn to Heidelberg and then Dedesdorf. Ahh, wonderful Dedesdorf. We saw five storks on a roof. Lover put up his hand and yelled "Stay!" I applauded.

Jan and Stan put us on a ship to cross the Baltic Sea to Copenhagen. In Copenhagen we visited a friend's 200-year-old house — thatched roof and all — picked cherries and I delighted our friend by teaching her how to make a pie! It's my very own method and recipe. You throw the pie crust at the wall. Tremendous way to relax the dough. My friend was thrilled. "Better Homes and Gardens" wanted to buy it, but of course I turned them down. Real art is not for sale I always say.

The time in Denmark was too short and on August 7 Lover and I jetted back to our darling children. We brought them fabulous presents.

The children, by the way, are marvelous. Each has a personal letter from the President in recognition of the Bicentennial. I have it filed in their up-to-date baby books. They are all accomplished slalom skiers; can give mouth-to-mouth resuscitation; walk six to eight miles a day; let me do all their shopping because as they say, "Mother, your taste is impeccable;" are in bed each night at 8 and up by 6 for a jog and have handmade all their Christmas gifts . . . wrapped and tagged by August 27. They used their own money for supplies — naturally. I suspect one made me an African piano. I learned to play one perfectly, you know, about two years ago when we were on safari.

I returned to my work as executive secretary for the largest oil company in the world in September. Impressive title? Just means "flunky." Ha ha. And on October 20 I was off again to an important convention in Washington, D.C. While there I purchased a white mink to go with my brown. Lover always wanted me to have a pair. But, darn it, wouldn't you know . . . the Secretary of State mussed the White when he hugged me at the airport. These politicians!

Oh, one more thing. While we were weekending in Utah, we

dropped in to see Bob Redford.But naughty, jealous Lover . . . when Bob came to the door, held up his hand and said "Stay." For some reason Redford applauded.

There's still a lot to look forward to this year and next year should be fantastic. Can hardly wait to hear YOUR exciting news." . . .

Oh yes, that is what I'd like to write.

But I probably won't. I'll probably tell the truth . . . just like I do every year. Well, ALMOST the truth.

Now take a look at the real Christmas letter . . .

THE REAL CHRISTMAS LETTER — OH HUM!

Receiving our REAL Christmas letter does not exactly mean the recipient is in for an electric afternoon of fascinating and appealing reading. More than likely, the reader will yield to yawns long before the second paragraph.

"Let's face it," I told my husband, "we are a dull family."

"Good!" he answered.

"We have no adventure in our souls," I said, "no daring, no lust for larks, no itch we haven't scratched. What will I put in our Christmas letter this year?"

"Tell it like it is," he advised.

Oh, my!

So here it is . . . like it is . . .

"Hi there:

Do hope you have had as dull a year as we have. If you didn't, don't write and tell me about it.

We spent a month this past Spring enjoying our annual "digs" . . . in the front yard, the side yard and the backyard . . . spading dandelions and burrowing for nightcrawlers. You know what they say — "The family that scoops together, stays together." That's what they say.

Shortly after that we drove Augie-Doggie to the vet and the children to the doctor to be treated for ringworm. Thus we began a very different sort of summer vacation.

Old Dad and I spent two days touring the basement hunting the extension cord for the air conditioner. We discovered many interesting things about one another during this period. I discovered he has an enlarged and colorful vocabulary — peppered with adjectives about wives who put things away and cannot find them. He discovered I often kick things that do not move quickly out of my way. His shin is healing nicely and the doctor says blood poisoning probably will not set in at this late date.

We bought two light bulbs and had the car greased in July. In comparison, August was quite monotonous.

Early in September the 10-year-old skinned his knuckles, the 15-year-old chipped a tooth and I lost my contacts. Old Dad and I spent two days touring the plumbing system in the bathroom, exploring the garbage disposal unit and raking the carpet. I heard that language again. But since I couldn't see there was little I could do.

I kicked out once but caught my big toe on the doorknob. The doctor said only three tiny bones were broken and I should be out of the cast by February. Certainly saves on socks. Ha ha.

I took up gourmet cooking this past year. I signed up for some classes but the teacher quit after the first session. She didn't say why. But who needs her. I just plunged ahead. We have had some delightful dinners. At least I thought they were. Old Dad didn't say. Poor thing, he really hasn't been feeling well lately. Goes to the doctor a lot. Has stomach problems, I guess. I told him he shouldn't eat between meals . . . just save up for dinner. He sort of groaned and stroked his gall bladder.

We had a blizzard. That was a thrill. The lights went out and everything. I tell you — the excitement was overwhelming. I couldn't take many titillating hours like that.

The children are fine. Our youngest stopped biting her nails three weeks ago, the sophomore was made hall monitor for the day and our oldest boy polished his shoes for the first time. He performed brilliantly. We are all so proud of him. I suppose this means he is finally growing up.

We have had quite a few interesting visitors over the year . . . the meter man, the mailman and the Avon lady who calls regularly. They don't stay long, but it is nice to have them pop in and out.

Old Dad and I spent two days touring the neighborhood looking for Augie-Doggie. It turned out to be the highlight of our year. You can't imagine the interesting things we saw in our neighbors' windows. Indescribable! Even Old Dad was speechless and had to admit it was a fun thing to do. We're looking forward to a repeat next Spring or Summer.

Oh, by the way, I go to the supermarket about once a week. Sometimes twice. This keeps me hopping, I can tell you. Just push that cart, load those boxes, unload those sacks, stock those cupboards . . . busy, busy, busy. I don't know where the time goes — just flys by on little mouse feet.

Which reminds me of another adventure. The snap of the trap often jollies up our evening hours and gives us something to do besides watch the tube.

Old Dad plans to retire when he is 105. With three children in college and two more scheduled, he thinks this is a reasonable age to shoot for, I can hardly wait. We have such mad plans for his retirement.

That just about wraps up our year. I can hardly wait to see what next year brings. If it doesn't improve, I can tell you one thing. I'm certainly not going to write another one of these silly letters."

THINKING THIN THROUGH HOLIDAYS

It is my honest opinion that holidays were created for only one type of person . . . skinny!

I am almost sure that the first Christmas angel weighed 98 pounds dripping wet. Why else would we celebrate with plum puddings and cookies and goose and whipped sweet potatoes? Have you ever seen a low-cal peppermint candy cane?

Not once have I ever heard Santa say . . . "Ho Ho Ho . . . how about a carrot stick?"

And Rudolph isn't sitting around drinking vegetable juice either. He didn't get that red nose from drinking V-8, I can tell you that.

I have to admit that Santa isn't what you call a sweet, thin thing. He's pretty heavy . . . I know that. But he doesn't have social pressures hanging over his head . . . no one expects Santa Claus to be a sex symbol. He's just Santa. Fat, jolly and rich!

Personally, I envy him. He doesn't have to worry about finding a holiday dress to wear to parties — he just wears the same old thing year after year. Same size, same color, same old black belt and boots. He doesn't even change his hair style. He hasn't lost or gained a pound in years. You'd think with all those cookies and milk he'd put on a little. I know I certainly have. I know I certainly can't wear the Christmas dress I had back in 1954. Come to think of it . . . I don't want to. I think it was probably a maternity dress. I looked more like Santa then and was more comfortable. But that's another story. Another Christmas miracle.

I hang back from Christmas cooking because I know that if I bake it . . . I'm going to eat it. It is as simple as that.

For years our children begged for a mouthwatering centerpiece for our Christmas table. For years they wanted me to make a gingerbread house — you know the kind — windows shuttered in icing, walls mortared with jelly beans, doorknobs made of chocolate chips, a thousand calories per square inch. I ate my way through that dream house in 10 minutes. After I destroyed the sugar-cube half-bath off the master bedroom and started munching the chimney I knew from that time forward I was going to stick to pinecones as centerpieces. Harder to digest but a lot less fattening.

Our children are complaining this year. So is my husband. So is Augie-Doggie. They are complaining that our kitchen smells like clorox instead of Christmas cookies. I tell them that clorox is not fattening — just antiseptic. We will have a clean Christmas this year I say — not a fat one.

"I am not going to make sugared nuts and pralines and fudge and divinity this year," I told them. "I am going to try something new. We will have a festive season — so do not worry — but it will be low in cholesterol. I will tip the lettuce leaves with red food coloring; sprinkle the cottage cheese with a bit of mustard for glitter, simmer our broccoli in bright red beet juice. It will be just fine. It will taste good."

I did not believe me. They did not believe me either.

They started a massive campaign. It was called "Operation Sugarplum." When I opened my dresser drawer I found a recipe for coconut bonbons; my spritz gun appeared in the medicine cabinet; my earrings were dipped in powdered sugar; the clothes hamper sprinkled with red crystal decors; the toes of my bedroom slippers were stuffed with dates; a marshmallow popped from the kneenex box; cinnamon candies were fused on the TV screen. I wouldn't have been surprised to see my husband come dancing into our bedroom dressed like the little Pillsbury doughboy. It was a concentrated effort to break down my resistance. I did not bend. I held on. I whipped up a succulent, sweet dish of green-tree spinach topped with celery seed.

Augie-Doggie moped in the corner, my husband moped in his chair, the girls moped in their rooms, the boys moped in our neighbor's kitchen. She was baking Christmas cookies. They know a good place to mope when they see one.

They were looking quite sad, I had to admit. And very hungry. It was not turning out a bit like I expected it to. No one even wanted to Christmas shop. They just wanted to hang around home and look at the colored pictures of food in the magazines. I started to worry that maybe I wouldn't have even one Christmas present under our tree.

"I wonder what Santa will bring me for Christmas this year," I hinted to my husband.

"How about a bushel of string beans," he snapped. He did not look like he was in a holiday mood. He was gnawing his knuckles and gazing at a picture of a mince pie. I began to feel sorry for him.

I began to see that I was the only one who could whip my family back into holiday happiness. I sneaked into our kitchen,

145

threw away the calorie-wheel, broke open the sugar cannister and dusted my hands with flour . . .

I was going to bake Christmas cookies after all!

I swear when I opened the oven door I heard "Jingle Bells."

THINGS CHRISTMAS MEANS

Never mind that the carpet's worn and the curtains don't match and that the one and only big, soft chair in the living room is dad's and 'you can't sit on it' — not even at Christmas time. Or that you might have to sleep on the couch without a pillow and a blanket from one of your little sisters and probably you'll have to share it with the dog.

Never mind that the Christmas angel on top of the tree looks like she's smashed and the string of lights blink sporadically and sometimes not at all and the Christmas tree is not a flocked beauty but a green Scotch spotted across the tree lot by your mother because it "talked to her" and she answered. She answered by picking that very one — another orphan tree just like last year's — flat on one side, empty of branches in the middle and puny on top, but just like last year's turning into a 'magic' tree the minute the family gathers about. I wonder how that always happens?

Never mind that the smells from the kitchen remind you of Smoky the Bear and the plum pudding is made from a box mix — or that someone ate most of the Christmas goodies, leaving only the pink sugar-coated figs, or that the fudge has thumb prints and no nuts and the peanut brittle turned lime green for the third Christmas in a row.

Never mind, Christmas means home.

CHRISTMAS MEANS MEMORIES

Memories of Christmases past, of seven little bodies all in new Christmas Eve pajamas that fit, tearing up the stairs, down the stairs and around the stairs on Christmas morning pretending awe and surprise, strictly for mom and dad's bene-fit, at the pile of presents beneath the tree. Pretending awe and surprise at presents they already knew they had — presents they knew they had because the designated "flashlight kid" had played his beams over them during the night and reported back "You gotta' doll, you gotta' bike, you gotta' big truck and I gotta' Mr. Machine."

Memories of the ultimate fate of poor Mr. Machine, memories

that remain a dark and dreaded secret in the family archives only to be brought to light when someone wants to blackmail a brother . . . memories.

Memories of dad in his nightshirt patiently assembling the millions of pieces of plastic associated with a dollhouse advertised as "partially assembled." The only thing assembled was a tiny lampshade perched on a lamp. At 2 a.m. dad announces to a snow-filled world "No more dollhouses" and then promptly has four more daughters and eventually four more dollhouses. Memories of mom, in her apron, coming unglued, nerve by nerve as Christmas approaches and then passes and miniature rubber soldiers, tinker toys and Barbie Doll shoes appear in the jello, the potty chair and the oven. Christmas means memories.

CHRISTMAS MEANS FAMILY

Cold noses and mixed-up mittens, a special stocking for Augie-Doggie, Christmas Eve at Grandma's with everyone. Our own special surprises and secrets, our own special angel in the Christmas program at church . Our family angel, her halo shining, her wings on straight, her hands folded in an angelic pose and her tongue sticking out as she passes her brothers seated on the front row pew . . . ruining her image and my reputation.

Christmas means family and the additions that seem to keep coming and coming. A son-in-law who is adjusting and becoming not an "in-law" but just a son and two very special little girls that bring Santa back into our house where he belongs — and where, actually, he never left.

A family that is cast under a spell at Christmas time. Sisters who cannot stand brothers, brothers who abhor sisters suddenly become good, fast friends. No name calling, no hair pulling, no routs at the dinner table . . . "Joy to the World" says mother. "Peace on Earth" sighs dad . . . it lasts 24 hours and it is truly glorious. It is Christmas.

CHRISTMAS MEANS LOVE

Love coming from that first tiny Christmas tree grabbed up on Christmas Eve many years ago . . . the last one in front of the store . . . a Christmas tree that had an 'expectant' look and so did I as our first child was born a week later. After that the Christmas trees and our family grew and grew and grew as did the love that went with it.

Love means my husband, Lee, and our children and grandchildren . . . Karen and Dave, Angie and 'Chelle, Sue, John, David, Mary, Amy and Claudia . . . They join me on this Christmas Eve in wishing each of you a very, very Merry Christmas.